11-11: The Carl Fyler Story

Karl Webb and Ann Norlin

11-11: The Carl Fyler Story

Copyright ©2012 by Karl Webb and Ann Norlin

All rights reserved. With the exception of quoting brief passages for the purposes of review, no part of this publication may be reproduced without the prior written consent of the authors.

For more information contact the authors at:
Ditto Ink Publishing
dittoink@gmail.com

ISBN 9780615890791

Graphic Design by Rod Seel
Photos and letters from the collection of Dr. Carl J. Fyler

Proudly printed in the United States of America

CreateSpace

Dedication

This book is in honor and memory of S/Sgt. Joseph Robert Sawicki and all of the other unsung heroes that have made the ultimate sacrifice so that we may live in freedom.

Introduction

There seems to be a shortage of real heroes today. At least in the public eye, there seems to be a dearth of people who live their lives with integrity, true to their own ideals and the ideals of this country. Perhaps that is why we must learn to look at the stories of the real people who live nearby. It might be your dentist, your travel agent, or the person who lives next door. That is where the true heroes will be found.

11-11: The Carl Fyler Story, is one example of such a story.

Dr. Carl Fyler's story is one of a true American. His roots run deep in this country, as his family is one of the founding families of the nation. The Fyler's immigrated to this country in 1630, and have been history makers ever since. There is a long and proud line of Fylers that have defended and grown this country from the beginning.

Out of this stream came Major Carl Fyler, a well-known and respected B-17 bomber pilot from World War II. Carl flew with the Mighty Eighth Air Force's Hell's Angels. After 25 plus hazardous missions, Carl and his crew were shot down over Bremen, Germany on November 29th, 1943. Carl ended up as a prisoner of war in the infamous Stalag Luft 1, where he spent 510 days before returning to the United States, a changed man.

There are, of course, many men and women who shared in this story of courage, loyalty and heroism. Understandably, the war affected some in a negative way, but Carl's strength, courage and beliefs did not waiver. He too struggled with the after affects of his experiences, but in the end, he chose to take his experience of war and let it make him stronger, rather than break him.

11-11: The Carl Fyler Story is the story of a man who let adversity, sorrow, betrayal and hardship form him into a man who fought for what was right. He learned to mark time as needed, but to never, ever, ever give up.

This book is as authentic of a biography as one might find. It is based in its entirety on actual documents, oral interviews, and from the personal belongings of Carl J. Fyler. Much of the story is told in his own words. The italicized sections in the text are from actual letters written by the person speaking. Other sections are excerpts from Major Fyler's own book, *"Staying Alive,"* published in 1996. The bolded sections are taken from other published resources, found cited at the conclusion of the book.

This is an inspiring and true story of a real hero. We hope you will enjoy reading it as much as we did writing it.

Karl Webb
Ann Norlin

Beginnings

The room at the Veteran's Administration long-term care facility was spartan. There was nothing comforting or home-like about the cold tile floors and the sparse furnishings that consisted of a hospital bed, a dresser and a TV that echoed in the bare room. Carl Fyler lay in this bed and looked at the institutional walls around him. It wasn't the first time he had to mark time by staring at walls, held in a place against his will. It was almost like the solitary confinement he had experienced in Nazi Germany more than 60 years before. The irony of the situation was not lost on him. Once again he was fighting for his life, and not just his own. This time, he was fight for his wife Marguerite as well.

He had come to the VA willingly enough. He had, after all, been starving to death, and fighting to get the VA to realize that for more than a year now. At first, he merely choked more frequently than usual, but things had progressed to the point where he could not keep any food down. He would go to the VA outpatient clinic where they would poke and prod and scope, then send him home with prescriptions for acid reflux and instructions to return in three months. Didn't they understand? He couldn't get the food down! He wasn't able to take in enough calories to sustain him! He had lost 80 lbs. in a little over a year, more than he had lost during the whole time he had been a POW. He was starving to death in his own home.

Carl's memory of those few months was dark around the edges. As he became more and more malnourished, his mind had gotten more and more fuzzy. He did remember that several women from his church were taking turns bringing him soup and tapioca and nutrition shakes, as these went down easier than anything else, but it was of no avail. He was growing weaker and weaker. He knew that at the rate he had been going, he would have been gone by Thanksgiving. He had fallen numerous times, and then didn't have the strength to get back up. Once he had fallen in the back yard and lay there for hours before he could get up, with the black ants biting him. His pastor had been putting pressure on him to contact his nephews in Tulsa, Oklahoma, but he had been reluctant. He wrote to his nephews all the time, and they to him, but he had not let them know just how bad things were getting. It was hard to admit he needed help, even to himself.

"No, I don't want to bother them," he said to the pastor. "They're busy with their own lives and I don't want to be a burden to them." His nephews were the sons of his beloved sister Gloria. He and Gloria had been through so much together over the years. Who would have thought she would have passed on so many years before he did? He sighed. He knew that if Gloria were still alive, he could turn to her for help, like he frequently had in the past.

Finally, toward the end of October, the VA hospital admitted him. Carl could have gone to the civilian hospital, but he chose to go to the VA. He had been willing to give up everything for love of his country. He had earned the right to be taken care of by that country.

The VA told him they were going to do surgery to insert a stomach tube to bypass what was believed to be a blockage in his esophagus.

Carl thought this would be a temporary measure and he would be home again soon, but he had been wrong.

His housekeeper had brought him to the VA hospital, where he was given a room and then he waited. There seemed to be some confusion as to when and how the surgery would be done, and he grew weaker still. Meanwhile, Marguerite was home alone, and this was a great worry to him. How could she manage on her own? He knew the compassionate women from the church were taking turns going to check on her, but still she shouldn't be alone. Carl was despondent. There was no one to turn to; no one to trust, and he didn't have the energy to fight any more. He had not been this low since the days just after the war.

Finally, Carl was sent by the VA to a local hospital for the placement of the stomach tube. He would later learn that his friend, the United States Senator, with whom he had worked on veteran's rights issues for so long, had become aware of his predicament and intervened on his behalf. At long last Carl would be able to take in nourishment again. But as he lay on the cold surgery table he had never felt more alone in his life. He worried about Marguerite. She was his faithful and loving companion and he missed her. He began to worry about what would happen to her if he died. He had not really considered that he might go first. He had drawn up a trust, but he wasn't sure if he had done everything he needed to do to put his house in order. The worry rolled over him in waves. He was afraid, not for himself, but for Marguerite. Carl had become justifiably concerned that there were those who were out for his money, and he knew they would go through her to get it.

As Carl lay in the pre-op room thinking these thoughts, the door had opened and his pastor had entered the room. He had never been so happy to see someone. She sat down next to him and held his hand as he poured out to her his concerns for his wife. At last they came to take him to surgery. She said a prayer with him, and then they wheeled him away.

When Carl awoke again, he was back at the VA. As he looked at the tube in his abdomen he realized that he was as dependent upon it now as he had been to the oxygen lines back in that B-17 bomber he still flew in his dreams. That is how he ended up in this place, separated from his wife, pondering his life. As he lay there, marking time, one hour blending into another, his mind began to wonder ...

****

As the haze cleared, he saw his beloved grandfather, Carlton P., sitting in a chair on the porch, looking off into the wide flat distance of the western Kansas prairie. Carl realized he was at his grandparent's house, a place he had been many times as a boy. He and his grandfather were close, and he loved nothing more than to sit with him on that porch and hear the stories of the past. He was surprised to find himself with his grandfather again ... so many years had passed since Carlton had left them. But he didn't question things; he just settled back into the chair and listened again to the Fyler family stories he had heard so many times before. It was nice to hear Grandfather's voice again ...

Lt. Walter Fyler was a man that captured young Carl's imagination from the start. Grandfather would say: The three children of Roman Fyler of Cornwall, England, Walter, George and Anne, and a grandson, George, Jr., decided they wished to go to the new land and worship the way they saw fit. So, in March of the year 1630 they boarded the tall sail ship the "Mary and John," in a company of 140

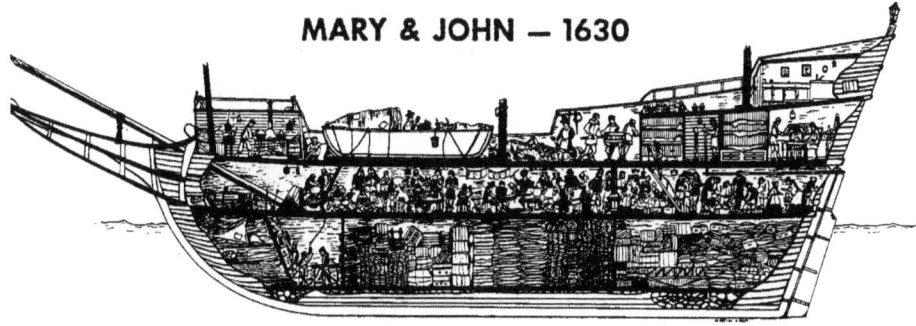

MARY & JOHN — 1630

persons. They began their journey at Plymouth England. They arrived in the New World seventy days later, on May 30, 1630, at the mouth of what is now Boston harbor. The ship's captain refused to sail up the Charles River as planned, because he feared running the ship aground in waters for which he had no chart. He instead left the passengers off the ship in a desolate locale miles from their intended destination. The settlers were forced to transport 150,000 pounds of livestock, provisions and equipment 20 miles overland to their final destination. Once there, they found good pasture for their cattle at Mattapan, now known as Dorchester Neck."

Walter was a lieutenant in the British Army. The Army in the New World was given the task of dealing with the Pequot Indians that lived in the area.

"The conflict that developed between the natives and the settlers was the first of many. In 1637 an actual war broke out between the Pequots and New England settlers. The Pequots were a warlike tribe centered along the Thames River in southeastern Connecticut. By 1630, under their chief, Sassacus, they had pushed west to the Connecticut River. There they had numerous quarrels with colonists, culminating in the murder by the Pequots of a trader, John Oldham, on July 20, 1636. On Aug. 24 Gov. John Endicott of Massachusetts Bay Colony organized a military force to punish the Indians, and on May 26, 1637, the first battle of the Pequot War took place when the New Englanders, under John Mason and John Underhill, attacked the Pequot stronghold near present-day New Haven, Conn. The Indian forts were burned and about 500 men, women, and children were killed. The survivors fled in small groups. One group, led by Sassacus, was caught near present day Fairfield, Conn., on July 28, and nearly all were killed or captured. The captives were made slaves by the colonists or were sold in the West Indies. Sassacus and the few who escaped with him were put to death by Mohawk Indians. The few remaining Pequots were scattered among other southern New England tribes." (4)

Walter was given a piece of land for services rendered during the war, on which he built a house that still stands today. In later years Carl and Marguerite had gone to see the Fyler House, which is currently the home of the Windsor Historical Society in Windsor Connecticutt. Carl admired the beautiful old house, which Walter had built himself.

And here it stood, on a lovely little plot of land that ran down to the river, hundreds of years later. As he stood in the house, Carl thought of the hardships the family faced in the new land. He imagined the forests that went for miles, the lack of food, the disease, and fighting the Indians. It all seemed such a grand adventure. He was from good Pilgrim stock!

****

Grandfather's stories of Lt. Walter Fyler's exploits in the new world were perfect fodder for young Carl's adventurous mind. He could be found crawling on his stomach in the grass in front of Grandfather's porch, popgun in hand, as he became Walter Fyler, protecting the settlers from wild animals and Indians. He had spent many days as a child re-living Grandfather's stories of Lt. Walter Fyler. He was proud that a man such as the lieutenant was one of his ancestors, that his blood and the man who was one of the founding fathers of his country ran intermingled.

****

The fact that true red, white and blue American blood flowed through Carl Fyler's veins is one that can be verified with a further walk through this country's history. There was Roger Fyler, who fought in the French and Indian War (1754-1758) and the Revolutionary War (1775-1783.) He lost a leg in the Battle of Long Island, a wound he survived, only to die two weeks after he got home of small pox. There was Paris Fyler, who commanded the sloop Hero that fought the British with two guns and 16 privateers. There were John and George Fyler who were two of the infamous Knowlton Rangers. The Knowlton Rangers were named after their commanding officer Thomas Knowlton. They were the first-ever American special operations force, sent in to gain information from the British in New York City. This group was a forerunner to the modern day CIA. Famous American spy Nathan Hale was also a part of this elite group of courageous men. Carl's relatives had helped to found a country, and so when the War Between the States broke out, his family was not about to let that country be torn asunder. The history books show Fyler after Fyler who fought on the side of the Union. There was George, Michael, Jacob, Jerome, Lemuel, Wallace and Orsarnus Fyler who wore the Union Blue. The Fylers fought valiantly in such historic battles as Yorktown, Williamsburg, Petersburg, Slash Church, Spotsville, Gettysburg and Appomattox. Carl was proud to say that his ancestors served under commanders such as Maj. Gen. Phillip Sheridan, Brig. Gen. George Meade and the great Ulysses S. Grant. It was Orasarnus Fyler who stood with Grant's battle weary men on the lawn at the courthouse in Appomattox in the spring of 1865 when the Southern States' famous General Robert E. Lee signed the surrender treaty that ended the Civil War.

No, the Fyler family was not one that was afraid to stand up and fight, and Carl took deep pride in that fact.

The scene in his mind shifted back to his childhood.

****

It was exciting for a young boy to grow up where the Wild West began, in the small community of Spearville, near Dodge City, Kansas.

Dodge City grew up just outside of Ft. Dodge, a military post placed to protect settlers from the Indians. In addition, the buffalo hunters who fed the railroad and the country's desire for buffalo hides were operating out of Dodge. By 1872, the shiny steel rails of the Atchison, Topeka and the Santa Fe railroad rolled into town, sparking even more growth as the cattle trade moved in with the railroad. By 1876 Dodge City was well known for lawlessness and gun slinging. Buffalo hunters, cowboys, railroad workers, drifters and soldiers were just some of the patrons of the saloons, gambling houses and brothels in the town of Dodge. Gunfights were not uncommon. The people of Dodge soon began to fear for their lives and so they hired Wyatt Earp. Four assistant deputies were also hired including another famous lawman of the Wild West, Bat Masterson, Wyatt's old buffalo hunting friend. Earp instituted a gun-toting rule that said carrying a gun was unlawful, and was in effect around the clock. Anyone found wearing a gun was immediately jailed. Soon, Dodge City's jail was filled. Everyone knew that it was not wise to draw a gun on Earp or his deputies. That action could have lethal consequences. By 1879, Dodge City had been tamed and Wyatt Earp had moved on to Tombstone Arizona where he would have a shoot out in the OK Corral.

Young Carl loved to imagine that he was the hot shot Earp. He would don his toy six shooters and walk up the dusty street, his white hat on his head, his guns in his holster at his side, waiting to be instantly ready for him when he reached for them. He would take on any lawless bandit that came into town. That's what the good people of Dodge City had hired him to do. Suddenly, the hairs on the back of his neck stood up, his intuition screaming out a warning. In a flash, his hands went to his guns and they came out of the holster, already blazing

But there was more to Carl's family history in the Wild West! While Wyatt Earp and the other gunslingers were cleaning up the Wild West, Carl's grandfather Carlton, found himself to be an orphan. The 13 children of George and Elisa Fyler were dispersed out to many families, a great tragedy after both parents died within months of each other. The youngest child, Carlton, then 4 years old, was taken in by a family named Mudd. The family soon moved to a farm near Abilene, Kansas where Carlton was raised. Abilene began as a stagecoach stop in 1857. The town grew quickly when Joseph G. McCoy decided to use the town for the point at which he could ship the cattle driven up from Texas to markets in the east via the newly run railroad lines in Kansas. In 1867 McCoy, a cattle buyer recently from Illinois extended the Chisholm Cattle Trail from Wichita, Kansas north to Abilene, Kansas. McCoy was able to make his wild scheme happen, and Abilene became the very first "cow town" of the west and enhanced the legend of the American cowboy. Like Dodge City, Abilene went from being a peaceful town to a town full of saloons and brothels during cattle season. McCoy and other town officials soon found themselves hiring gunslingers such as Wild Bill Hickok to provide the same services for their town as Wyatt Earp and Bat Masterson provided for Dodge. Another key player in the city of Abilene was Thomas Kirby, a banker who helped McCoy procure the money for his ventures. The Fylers and the Kirbys and the McCoys were soon intermarried. In 1883 Carlton Fyler married the schoolteacher, Florence Emily Kirby. They had 5 children - Eleanor, John, Charlotte, Lawrence and William. When the economy took a downturn in the

1890s, Carlton decided he needed to find a new career. Several of his brothers-in-law were dentists, and this was a career that looked good to him, and so he packed his family up and moved them to Kansas City, where he attended dental school. Carlton P. Fyler became a traveling dentist. Carl could just picture his grandfather in his mind, loading up his buggy with his kit and heading down to Abilene, where he would climb aboard the train. From there he would ride up and down the rail line, providing dental services for all the citizens of the small towns along the line. Finally, one such town in far western Kansas, LaCrosse, offered him free office space and a bit of land for a house if he would stay and be the town dentist. LaCrosse was a nice little town, and Florence agreed. The couple packed their belongings and moved their family west.

Son John had his own adventures in settling the west. As a young adult, he took over his brother Lawrence's homestead in Finney County, Kansas. The soft earth and the strong grass made perfect building materials in a nearly treeless land, and so like many of the early settlers John first lived in a house made of sod bricks, known as a soddie. Later he moved to town and went to work in a store called "The Bargain Store." One day a beautiful young woman came into the store with the Dvorak family, who ranched outside of town. John was immediately taken with her. Upon inquiring he learned that she was Lyda  Dvorak's sister Helen, from Wisconsin. John knew that she was the girl he wanted to marry. He began to court her, via letter, after she went back to Wisconsin. Eventually she agreed to be his wife, and came back to Kansas to stay.

And so the blood flowed down the line until at last, Carl John Fyler was born on May 14, 1921 the firstborn child of John and Helen Fyler. Sister Gloria Amelia would follow in September of 1924.

****

Carl stirred from his memories when the nurse came in to bring him "dinner," which consisted of a can of thick milky substance that poured into the tube. He would have much preferred a juicy steak. The tube had plugged up three times already, and they had had to take him back over to the hospital and reinsert a different sized tube each time. Carl grimaced as he watched the liquid glug into the tube. Between the problems with the tube and the fact that he could never again eat a decent meal, he had begun to wonder if the whole process was worth it. On top of all that, he had developed a dehabilitating cough that he couldn't seem to shake. The coughing spells would come, causing him to hack and choke until he was breathless. Sometimes even the slightest exertion brought on one of the spells. As the nurse left, he leaned over to pick up the TV remote, which triggered a coughing fit that left him gasping for air. Although his Fyler nature would cause him to fight until the very end, Carl was becoming aware of the fact that the end was indeed near. When he could move again, he used the remote to turn on the television. He flipped through the channels until he came to the History Channel, where he stopped. Carl had always been a student of history. He was fascinated by the stories of the past. He also kept up on all the current events of the day. Except for the time when he had been so ill, his mind was still as sharp as it had ever been, and he intended to keep it that way. He knew he would need his wits for what was about to come.

The History Channel was running a show on the Dust Bowl Era of the 1930s – the dirty thirties eh? Carl remembered those all too well. He had lived in the middle of that infernal bowl himself. As the announcer droned on, Carl once more drifted back …

****

Spearville was on the high plans of Western Kansas, a semi-arid region in the rain shield of the Rocky Mountains. One could travel for many miles before spotting a tree, and even then it was often a scraggly excuse for one. When only the Indians and the buffalo were there, the grasses held the soil in place. But as the settlers moved in

and their plows tore up the grass, conditions began to change. With the grasses gone, there was nothing to hold down the topsoil. The name Kansas means "people of the south wind." The state had been aptly named. The south and west winds did blow, almost constantly, and soon it was carrying the loose topsoil along with it. Growing drought conditions throughout most of the 1930s only made matters worse.

Carl would never forget the day the first big dust storm rolled into Spearville. It was on April 14, 1935 – Palm Sunday. It grew dark, almost as if a tornado was approaching, but it wasn't a stormy day. He and Gloria were in the yard when they suddenly became aware of the encroaching darkness. They looked at each other in alarm as the phone began to ring inside the house. After a few minutes Helen came out on the porch. "Carl, Gloria, come into the house," she said. They followed her in, as the dust enveloped their home. They went from window to window to look out, but they could see nothing but gray from the dust. They tried to listen to the radio, but even it had gone silent. It really seemed like the end of the world. John Fyler finally decided to lead his family into the cellar. There the dust entombed them for over four hours that afternoon, and it was days before the dust settled entirely. But it wasn't gone. It was in everything, got into every crack. Soon they were eating the dust and sleeping in the dust. It was in their hair and all their clothes. Even the plates inside of the cupboards had so much dust on them a person could write their name in it. Carl remembered that his mother would go in a frenzy about all the dust in her house and she would make Gloria help her clean until Gloria cried about how she hated all that dust. And still it was there. They would no sooner get the house close to clean before another dust roller would hit them again.

Carl remembered one frightening night when a dust storm rolled in just after his father left the store to come home for dinner. It got so dark that John could not see – a brown blizzard of dust. He felt his way along the edge of the houses, counting houses until he came to his own. They were never so happy as when John blew in the door in a cloud of dust, safe.

Farmers in Kansas, Oklahoma, Texas, Colorado and Nebraska took a double hit during the 1930s because in October 1929, the stock market collapsed. All of a sudden, people became afraid to leave their money in the bank. There was a run on the banks, with frantic people pulling out every cent they had, causing banks to fail all over the country. The collapse triggered a depression the likes of which the country had not seen before. In one year's time, the unemployment rate in the United States doubled. Many people were out of work, people who had always been gainfully employed and had large families. It was a very difficult time.

The Dust Bowl and the Depression were hard times for the people of Spearville. Their farms were quite literally blowing away and there were no other jobs to be had. Many families packed up and left, hoping to find greener fields elsewhere. Because Father was the storeowner he was able to keep food on the table for his small family, but it was not so for many of their friends and neighbors. Carl knew there were many times his mother had handed part of their supper out the back door to people traveling through, looking for work. Carl recalled seeing their haunted, vacant faces as they looked in the door at their modest house. He wondered at the time what it must feel like to be so hungry you would knock on a stranger's door to beg for food. He would remember those

people later, when he was that hungry himself. Carl was also pretty sure, looking back on things, that John Fyler let people buy in the store on credit that he knew they could never repay. Finally the times hit home, and John lost the store. John was a man of great integrity, and he refused to let his debtors come up empty handed. Bit by bit, he paid them all back in full, at times to the detriment of his own family. For this, Helen never really forgave him.

But for Carl and Gloria, things never seemed too bad, especially since John and Helen worked very hard to make their lives as normal as possible. However, things that previously had been readily available, now were either not available or there was no money to buy them with. Carl and Gloria learned to make do. They would save used items and find other uses for them. Nothing was ever thrown away or wasted.

Beyond that, their childhood was a good one. Helen's family lived close by, and the siblings loved going over to play with cousins and to be doted on by their aunts. Gloria had a passion for painting and drawing, and from an early age she had a beautiful singing voice. Carl loved to fish and hunt and there was plenty opportunity for both. His favorite pastime was to explore the countryside, where he found all manner of interesting things, including fossils and Indian arrowheads. Each time he picked up an arrowhead, he imagined a battle between some Indian tribe and the army men from

Fort Dodge. In his mind's ear he could hear the cries of the men, the clank of the livery on the horses, the war whoops of the Indians and the din of the great battle. He knew he held a piece of history in his hand. Yes, life was good for a boy. And so he grew, tall and dark and handsome.

Carl loved school. At age 4 he pestered his father so often to take him to school that John Fyler finally went to the school and convinced them to let Carl start early. While he was not the best student in the school in terms of homework and tests and grades, Carl loved to learn and soaked up knowledge like a sponge. He was also very social, a natural-born leader. The other children gravitated to him. And in what seemed like a wink of an eye to Helen Fyler, her son, Carl Fyler, the apple of her eye, was in high school.

****

The strands of Glen Miller's 1939 hit "Moonlight Serenade" were drifting through Carl's mind. The waves of music carried him back to his Senior Prom ... he could feel the girl pressed close to him, smell her perfume, even though he could no longer see her face ... but he could feel the movement of their dance ...

The Senior Prom was the highlight of a wonderful four years for Carl. They were in many ways the best four years of his life. He was in his element. Carl had grown into a handsome teenager who was friendly and gregarious and well liked by all his classmates. At six feet tall and 165 lbs he was a natural for the football team, where he played tackle. Carl loved to sing, and sang in glee club and men's chorus. He also played trumpet for the Spearville High School band. He enjoyed that very much. Carl went to State level High School Music competitions in both voice and trumpet, and did well in both. Carl was also quite the thespian. His outgoing nature put him at ease on the stage, and he took on leading roles in nearly every play and operetta that Spearville High produced in the four years he was there. In his mind his high school days were a fun blur of football practices and games and music practice and play practices, clowning around with the guys and laughing with the girls at the sundry counter on Main Street, and stealing kisses from the girls at dances. He remembered clearly the day he graduated. He looked out across the faces and saw his parents, bursting with pride. He was glad they were pleased with him. They had worked hard to get him to that place and, though he was sad to be moving on, he knew he had a bright future ahead of him. He wasn't sure what he wanted to do in life, but whatever it was he would be the best at it! Carl was amazed at his own youthful optimism.

But even that young Carl knew the Nazis were running roughshod over Eastern Europe in 1939. There was a dark cloud on the horizon of his future, which was now his past. He sighed as the joy of those memories flooded over him. He never saw most of those kids again, and many of the boys were lost at war. The Serenade came back and swirled around him, as he held the girl in his arms. What was her name? Ah well, it didn't matter ... Marguerite was now his dance partner for life anyway ...

There were indeed dark clouds over Europe when Carl Fyler graduated in May 1939, just days before his 18th birthday.

World War I had drawn to a close just before Carl was born, but it had left unresolved many of the issues that had started it. Many of the democratic governments in Central and Eastern Europe were unstable and easily disturbed. Germany was one of those governments. The effects of the economic depression that Carl and Gloria experienced in Spearville, Kansas were felt worldwide, and those effects toppled the fragile democracy in Germany. The deteriorating economic conditions allowed, in 1933, the National Socialist German Workers party

– The Nazis, headed by Adolph Hitler – to come into power. This party was extremely nationalistic. They put the welfare of Germany and of the party over all other considerations, moral or otherwise. Hitler's end game was to create "living space" for a master race he intended to create, and to dominate the world. He had a raging hatred of Jews, and had every intention of exterminating them as a race. Hitler was madly brilliant, and knew well how to play people and countries to his gain. He skillfully used the divisions between countries left over by the war to further divide potential opponents and to secure allies. He knew most countries would do most anything to avoid another war, and he used that knowledge to his advantage. Hitler quickly consolidated power, eliminated parliamentary government, and viciously squashed any opposition. By 1938, the evil beast that was the Third Reich thrived. During March 1938 Germany had taken Austria under its control. By March 1939, Hitler, by deceit and by force had taken Czechoslovakia and turned his sights on Poland, Germany's neighbor to the north. Although Britain and France had guaranteed the integrity of Poland, Hitler and Josef Stalin, dictator of the Soviet Union, signed a secret, mutual nonaggression pact in August 1939. This sealed the fate of Poland. Germany moved into the country on Sept. 1, 1939. Soviet troops then moved in from the East to claim their part of Polish territory, and World War II began in earnest.

Carl and Gloria, though young, were watching the situation in Germany perhaps closer than most. After all, their pen pal Hans lived near Bremen Germany. Carl had been given a pen pal as an assignment for German class in high school, and soon Gloria was writing him as well. They learned that Hans was a member of the Hitler Youth Corps. When Hitler came into power, he banned the Boy Scout organizations that were active in Germany and quickly replaced them with the Hitler Youth. The Corp continued with many Scouting activities, but changed their content and intention. The physical activity and sports training of a traditional scout program soon became very militaristic in nature. For example, many Hitler youth activities involved firearm training, assault course work, and lessons in military tactics. Of course Hitler wanted to use this organization to indoctrinate the youth of the country and to prepare the boys for military service. By December 1936, five million German youth were involved with the Corps, and by 1940 it had eight million members. Nearly every young male in Germany was involved in some way, some as young as 10 years old. As time passed Carl noticed that Hans' letters were less and less about sport and school and more and more about his activities with the Youth Corps. Hans even began to ask questions in his letters about military posts and activities in Kansas. Later, when Carl was dropping bombs on Bremen Germany, he would wonder if Hans was waiting below to receive them.

But as of 1939, America itself was largely uninterested in the war, more concerned with its own economic woes. America was maintaining a position of neutrality, and so Carl turned instead to wondering what to do with his life. There was no money for Carl to go to one of the big state universities, so Carl enrolled in the new Dodge City Community College with the intention of getting his teaching certificate. The college had first opened its doors in September 1935, housed in the upstairs of the Dodge City Senior High School building. But while Carl was attending classes, things were happening that would take him to a very different place …

****

Carl's attention moved to the present for a moment when he became aware of the sound of an airplane overhead. It was funny how, despite his hearing problems, he could almost always hear an airplane when it flew over, and he could usually tell what kind of plane it was too! He had kept up with aviation all these years, flown his own plane for a good number of them. Topeka's Forbes Field had been an Air Force base at one time, and as such had excellent runway space available to continue to train pilots on the latest aircraft. He cocked his damaged ears and listened closer. Hmm. Small private jet most likely. Flying. How he missed flying a plane, bomber or otherwise. Nothing better than to be up in a clear blue sky, soaring like a hawk over the prairie …

****

It seemed to Carl that the love of flying was buried deep in his DNA. Long before he ever went up in an airplane he had dreamed he could fly like the birds he watched as he laid in the grass as a youth, gazing into the sky and imagining his body in flight. He knew that his father shared those same dreams. He remembered with great fondness that as a youngster, whenever a plane flew over Spearville, he and his father would stop what they were doing and without a word stand side by side until the plane droned out of sight.

Those planes had not been flying over Spearville for very long by the time Carl came along in 1921. It was in 1907 that the two Wright brothers from North Carolina had made the first manned airplane that flew with any reliability. The new field of aviation had been born, and grew at an amazing rate in the next 10 years. By 1911 young aviators such as A.K. Longren from Topeka, Kansas, were making their own planes and barnstorming around the country.

Albin K. Longren was born into a Swedish family near Walsburg Kansas in 1882. The year was 1910 when Longren watched exhibition flyer J.C. Mars fly a plane called the Skylark near his home. Mars crashed the plane that day, and Longren helped him repair it. This sparked such a fascination for airplanes and for flying that soon he and a brother started building and selling airplanes out of a factory in Topeka. Their first creation was dubbed "Topeka" and on its test flight logged six miles in the air, just above the grass all the way. This earned Longren the distinction of being the first man to build and fly an airplane in Kansas. In order to raise enough money to continue

to build planes, Longren began performing for those who paid the price of admission. He performed air shows at fairgrounds in Kansas, Oklahoma and Nebraska. He was the self-proclaimed "Wizard of the Air." People would come out in droves, dressed in their Sunday best, to see the amazing feat of human flight. Unfortunately for Longren, the people could also sit outside the fairgrounds and watch the flight for free, hampering his fundraising efforts.

One day a young John Fyler had been riding his bike down a country road when he noticed a crowd gathered in a nearby field. Curious as to what was going on, John parked his bike, climbed under the fence, and walked over to the crowd. There he found a wonderful thing. A man, whom he believed was A.K. Longren himself, was building a real airplane in the field. John was enthralled as he watched the building of the aircraft, and then watched with exhilaration as the plane swooped, dived, and rolled over his head, and he was hooked. From that moment on, his fascination with flying was entrenched in his heart. This fascination was passed from father John to son Carl.

And so, when Carl went off to college and met an old man named Lester Fowler, who could fly the planes, he immediately arranged to have the man teach him to do the same. Carl spent hours with the man and his rickety plane, practicing taking off and landing in a barren field outside of Dodge City. Carl never forgot the feeling of those first flights ... the warm days, the wind hitting his face as he flew in the open-cockpit plane, sporting the leather helmet and aviator goggles. He never felt as happy and as free as he did when he was up in the sky, flying at what seemed an incredible speed, watching the ground below. It wasn't long at all before Carl had earned his pilot's license.

Carl had flown his own plane until he just couldn't do it anymore. It was with great reluctance that he had sold his last plane, a nifty little Piper Comanche. It was no wonder his old ears perked up at the sound of those planes going over. In his heart he was still that young man, flying over the prairie without a care in the world ...

****

In VA world, weekend evenings were the longest. The skeleton staff disappeared, and at times he felt like he was the only one in the whole building. Even the TV programs were terrible, and it left him with nothing to do but stare at the ceiling and think.

Tonight his thoughts went to Ellen Jean. Strange, he hadn't thought of her in ages. He had lost track of her many years ago. She seemed to be near him tonight though. For so many years he had harbored a raging anger at her, one that at times, in the beginning, had been like a forest fire, hard to control and likely to cause damage. But he had controlled his fury in the long run and he was glad that he had. He never saw Ellen Jean again, and as the years passed like a river under a bridge his anger flowed out and away with them. Now he thought of Ellen Jean with pity, and with a slight sadness that they had been nothing more than a mistake in each other's lives. He no longer harbored any anger or ill will toward her. He just wondered what had happened to her. His life since Ellen Jean had been wonderful. What had hers been like?

The years shifted, and he went back ...

****

There was something about Ellen Jean that caught his eye when Carl first saw her at the soda counter that day. He had just left class at Dodge City Community College and was stopping by the drug store for a soda with some friends before heading back home to study. The group he was meeting was sitting at the far end of the soda counter, laughing and cutting up as Benny Goodman's swinging band jumped in the jukebox behind them. They were a fun crowd and he was anxious to join them. But then dark-haired Ellen Jean caught his eye. She was sitting with a girlfriend at the near end of the counter. The two were talking with great animation, and Carl heard her infectious laugh ring across the room several times. Soon he found himself watching her. There was something about her, so much life in her, that he couldn't help himself. He noted that she was looking at him too. Once, to his embarrassment, she caught him staring. Ellen Jean waved at him, and red-faced, Carl waved back then tried doggedly not to look at her any more. However, when she got up to leave, he couldn't help but notice. To his surprise, instead of heading for the door she came back to his table with a captivating smile on her face. "Hi" she said pertly, "I think I know you. Aren't you in math class with me?" She stuck her hand out to shake his hand. "My name is Ellen Jean." Carl took her hand and shook it as their eyes met. She had such big brown eyes."Ah, why yes, I believe we do share a class. I am Carl, Carl Fyler, nice to meet you …" It was one of those moments in life that turned a person in a different direction forever.

After that chance meeting in the drug store, Carl and Ellen Jean became regulars around Dodge. Ellen Jean was tall and pretty in an arrestingly different way than the other girls Carl had dated. She was fun to be around. She made him laugh. She loved to dance to the sounds of the swing bands and the two of them spent many good nights dancing, their bodies in perfect rhythm with each other. Carl was completely smitten with Ellen Jean's vitality and love of life, and as for her part, she loved her tall, handsome boyfriend. She knew she looked good on his arm. Ellen Jean had come to college to catch a husband, and it seemed to her that Carl Fyler would do just fine. It was, for a time, a match made in heaven.

While the brash new pilot from Kansas was getting his first tastes of love and of the wild blue yonder in Dodge City, Kansas, the storm of war that had been raging in Europe was about to spread out of the confines of that continent and engulf the rest of the world.

Throughout 1940 and 1941, the Americans were still trying to convince themselves that the war that was grinding Europe into pieces didn't really affect them. Hitler was becoming more and more brazen, and the British were fighting their battles alone. But when the Japanese bombed Pearl Harbor, Hawaii on December 7, 1941, the ability of the United States to remain neutral in the war was blown out of the water as surely as the ships in the harbor that day.

"The Japanese attack on Pearl Harbor shook the United States as nothing had since the firing on Fort Sumter," wrote historian Samuel Eliot Morrison. Republicans and Democrats, interventionists and isolationists, labor and capital, closed ranks and the nation moved from peace to war with a unity that it had never known before in a time of crisis. On December 8, President Roosevelt appeared before a joint session of Congress to ask for a declaration of war against Japan. Congress responded with only a single dissenting vote. Three days later, Germany declared war on the United States, a decision more calamitous for its cause than its invasion of Russia the previous June.

At a high level meeting convened at the White House days after the attack, England's Prime Minister Winston Churchill and Roosevelt endorsed the "defeat Germany first" strategy agreed to earlier and called for an immediate buildup of airpower in Britain. The following month, General Hap Arnold, who had been instructed in flying by the Wright Brothers, created the Eighth Air Force. Arnold appointed General Ira Eaker and World War I veteran Charles Toohey Spaatz to organize an air force.

On February 4, 1942, Eaker and six new staff officers left for their new assignment in England, while Spaatz stayed in Washington to oversee the preparation and dispatch of the planes. This left the task of building an entire air force on foreign soil to Eaker, a 45-year-old newly minted general who had never had a large command. Eaker would work closely with the British RAF to assemble the infrastructure that would be essential for the Eighth Air Force's bombing operations." (1)

The Eighth would go from seven men and no planes in February of 1942, while Carl Fyler was learning to fly in the United States, to 185,000 men and 4,000 planes by December of 1943. The intent was to take these men and these planes deep into the heart of Germany and render it incapable of fighting a war. It was a daunting task indeed.

Carl remembered the bombing of Pearl Harbor as acutely as if it were yesterday. He could still fill the sinking sensation he felt in his gut as he sat next to the radio in his parents' living room. They all sat in stunned silence, listening to the reports of the bombing of the navy ships in the harbor of Honolulu, Hawaii by the Japanese Imperial Air Force. Carl thought of his lineage. Carl thought of all his ancestors who had fought to keep the world safe. Carl thought of his pilot's license. He knew what he had to do. Carl went and enlisted in the newly formed Army Air Corps.

****

He had never really stopped re-living the war. While the memories had mellowed over the years, they still flooded in on him when he least expected it, and the nightmares had never stopped. As he spent yet another day laying in the bed at the VA, he began to think about how the experience of living through the second World War, the one that was suppose to be the war to end all wars, had changed the world. It had changed everything, absolutely everything in his life. In some ways it had destroyed him, left him wrung out and lifeless, with a choice to start over again or not. Yet in another strange way it had made him strong, made him the man he was. He had spent the next 60 years trying to live with it and understand it and make peace with it. As Carl considered these things he began to drift back. Where had all the time gone? With the wisdom of an old man's inner eye, he began to reflect upon his life. It was a good life. There was so much to remember, and he could see it all in his mind, all like a new 1939 MGM Technicolor movie …

War

1942

The enlistment letter came in the mail, instructions for joining the Air Corps …

"Secure three letters of recommendation and a birth certificate, and be in Wichita, Kansas by January 29, 1942 at 8:00 a.m. at which time you will be physically and mentally examined by the Cadet Examining Board for eligibility for enlistment in the Air Corps as an Aviation Cadet. It will be necessary that you appear at the hour given above in order to enable the board to give you the required examinations.

"Whether or not the applicant has passed will be determined immediately by the Cadet Examining Board and, if successful, the applicant will enlist at once, be appointed an Aviation Cadet and sent to one of the three Air Corps Replacement Training Centers. There he will be given a physical examination for flying duty and further tests to determine the type of training he is to receive … For the successful aircrew candidate, flying training will last approximately seven and a half

months, during which time the Aviation Cadet will receive $75 per month, plus $1.00 per day subsistence. He also receives, at Government expense, lodging, necessary clothing, equipment, medical care and a $10,000 life insurance policy during the period of training. On assignment to active duty in the Air Corps Reserve, he receives $500 for each year of his active service ..." (letter, Carl Fyler Archives)

By the end of the day of January 29, 1942, Carl Fyler was an Aviation Cadet in the Army Air Corps.

Training for Cadets came in four stages. The Classification stage lasted a week. It was here the Army processed the cadet and issued him his equipment. This was the stage where it would be decided whether the cadet would train as a navigator, bombardier, or pilot. Carl, with his college degree and pilot's license, was immediately sorted as a pilot.

The education and training stages were nine weeks each. Each nine week stage was divided up into two, four and a half week halves: a lower half and an upper half. The lower half was made up of students just beginning the stage and the upper half of the class was made up of the students who were more than halfway finished with training. The idea was that more experienced cadets would help the new cadets get through the section before they were promoted to the next stage.

Pre-Flight stage was divided into two parts and was attended by pilots, navigators, and bombardiers. The first six weeks concentrated on athletics and military training. This was followed by three weeks of academics. They were taught the mechanics and physics of flight. The cadets were required to pass refresher courses in mathematics and physics. Then the cadets were taught to apply their knowledge practically by teaching those in the lower half of the class. They taught them aeronautics, deflection shooting, (which is shooting ahead of the target to compensate for the movement of the plane) and thinking in three dimensions.

Then it was on to Pilot School for Carl. It was the beginning of the most mentally demanding training program in the American military at the time.

"For pilots especially, selection and training had to be rigorous. They would not be handling a rifle, but a huge, highly complex weapon of immense cost and destructive capability. Before a pilot received his wings and commission as a 2nd Lieutenant, he went through three flight training schools – Primary, Basic and Advanced." (1)

Primary Pilot Training taught basic flight using two-seater training aircraft. Private flight schools that had contracted with the Army usually did this training. Cadets got around 60 to 65 Flight Hours in Stearman, Ryan, or Fairchild trainers before going to Basic. Basic Pilot Training taught the cadets to fly in formation, fly by instruments or by aerial navigation, fly at night, and fly for long distances. Cadets got about 70 Flight Hours before being promoted to Advanced.

Advanced Pilot Training placed the graduates in two categories: single-engined and multi-engined. Single-engined pilots flew fighters and fighter-bombers. Multi-engined pilots learned to fly transports and heavy bombers. First they flew Trainer aircraft, and then transitioned to front-line aircraft. Cadets were supposed to get a total of about 75 to 80 Flight Hours before graduating. Graduates were usually graded as Flight Officers (Warrant Officers). Cadets who graduated at the top of their class were graded as Second Lieutenant. By the time Carl went to war, he was a 2nd Lieutenant in the Army Air Corps.

Carl would be sent to the Chico training base in California for Basic Pilot School.

****

A smile moved across his face as Carl thought about his time at Chico. That was a good summer, one he would never forget. He hoped it was a good memory for Ellen Jean too, wherever she had ended up. The memories flooded back …

****

June 20, 1942

Dear Folks
I will be flying at night. I don't think that will be very easy. I have enough trouble flying the thing in the daytime, let alone at nighttime. I am learning how to fly on instruments and radio. I like this type of flying swell, only I correct too much. When I am supposed to push the nose down just a little, I do it too much and the same way when going up.

My instructor has a black hood that he covers the back seat with. I get under this and fly the plane, as he calls to me over the radio. I climb the plane up to about 7,000 feet then I try the "works" up there – not ever seeing a thing or where I am going. I fly upside down and do stalls and spins. Spins are a real thrill, when you can't see a thing. Often I fall 1,000 feet or more and hit 180-210 miles per hour. When you change direction of the plane you have to make easy turns, otherwise you will black out …

July 18, 1942
Last night I flew 1½ hours. I am so tired! All that I have left to do is fly across the country - 2 hours at night – a real hard trip. This afternoon I flew with Lt. Tanner on a check ride, and I passed it okay – so I feel rather happy. Yesterday my instructor said, "Mr. Fyler, where do you want to go to advanced training?"

Well I was surprised but I said, "Back to Arizona or Texas. I thought I might be nearer to home, although I do rather like California and its coast. Flying at night is great! The air is warm and smooth. The sky is full of stars and the earth is black as pitch except for the lights of town and of the airfield. A real sight, all colors and brightness. Of course I am real tired, fatigued. I fly day and night, with only about 6 hours of sleep. But I like it fine!

The relationship between Carl and Ellen Jean had heated up into a real romance. Carl remembered in his heart how deeply he had fallen for EJ's vivacious beauty. Sometimes it was like he drew his own energy from her. It was hard to be away from her and concentrate on his duties, and he looked forward to the time when she could come to California to be with him. At long last the time came:

July 20th, 1942
Dear Folks,
Ellen Jean should arrive tomorrow, and if all works out as I have planned, I will have Saturday afternoon and all day Sunday with her, and perhaps a few evenings this next week. Then next week will be our "graduation dinner dance." I have not told her about this, so it should be a pleasant surprise for her. We will have a big name dance band here. They will come from San Francisco, so it should be real nice.

It was nice to hold Ellen Jean in his arms again, and she looked beautiful the night of the dance. The warm California air and the ocean beating on the soft sand and the stars that made flying so incredible conspired together to create an intoxicating mix for the young couple. Perhaps at some level, they knew this time was fleeting, and therefore all the more precious. They spent every minute they possibly could together.

July 25, 1942
Ellen Jean arrived Saturday around noon, just after I got to town. I was so glad to see her. I gave her a 2-1/2 pound box of California fruit nut candy. (I got a real good deal!) She liked it very much. Then that evening we went out to dinner, to the best place in town, "The Southern." Our steaks cost $1.10 each. Generally we get a hamburger, but I decided we should have a good time, so we did.

Afterwards we went on a walk through the park, then we went to 2 cocktail lounges. I had her meet some of the other cadets and showed her the difference between officers and enlisted men. Then Sunday morning we went horseback riding up toward the hills, up to a little stream that we swam in ...

A few days later, on stationery that bore the logo of the swanky Hotel Mark Hopkins, Nob Hill, San Francisco

Dear Folks,
EJ and I are here in Frisco. Tomorrow we will go to Luke Field in Phoenix Arizona. I will write you more from there.
We saw the ocean, bay, and Golden Gate Bridge, Chinatown and are at best hotel in town. Great town, this ...

As trite as it sounded, Carl knew that he and Ellen Jean truly did leave their hearts in San Francisco that summer ...

Carl's next stop was Luke Air Field just outside of Phoenix, Arizona.

Luke Air Force Base is named for the first aviator to receive the Medal of Honor – Lt. Frank Luke Jr. Born in Phoenix in 1897; the "Arizona Balloon Buster" scored 18 aerial victories during World War I in the skies over France before being killed, at age 21, on Sept. 29, 1918.

In 1940, the U.S. Army sent a representative to Arizona to choose a site for an Army Air Corps training field for advanced training in conventional fighter aircraft. The city of Phoenix bought 1,440 acres of land, which they leased to the government for $1 a year.

During World War II, Luke was the largest fighter-training base in the Air Corps, graduating more than 12,000 fighter pilots from advanced and operational courses in the AT-6, P-40, P-51 and P-38, earning the nickname "Home of the Fighter Pilot."

Carl and Ellen Jean were married on Sept. 29, 1942 in Phoenix, Arizona with both sets of parents and sisters there. Carl sighed as he remembered that day. In retrospect he should have known there were going to be problems. Both sets of parents were against the marriage, and the tension in the room was palpable. Instead of a joy filled occasion, it was a stressful one. The two mothers had gotten into a confrontation that day. At that moment, Carl had wanted to call the whole thing off and elope with Ellen Jean later. He loved her, and he wanted to have someone to fight for, and for these reasons he tried to make peace between the women and get through the day. He hoped that perhaps his mother and Ellen Jean would learn to like each other over

time. He had been wrong. He should have followed his first instinct. If he had, things might have turned out differently. But he did not, and things went downhill from there.

After completion of the training at Chico, Carl was sent to Geiger Field in Washington State. Since they never really had a honeymoon, the long drive from Arizona to Washington State had served in that capacity. The memory of those days would always be sweet to him. He could feel Ellen Jean's arm hooked in his as they walked together through such wonderful places. It made him think of the song *"America the Beautiful."*

"O Beautiful for spacious skies, for amber waves of grain, for purple mountains' majesty, across the fruited plain."

They would stop and picnic along the road, laughing and happy during the day, and in sleep in each other's arms at night. It was good love while it lasted. It made him sad to think that those were the best of the days they would have together. Their hearts had been so full of hope when they had started out …

****

Our trip up here was swell. Ellen Jean and I saw some beautiful country. Grand Canyon, southern Utah, Salt Lake, the Mormon Tabernacle, Idaho, Butte Montana, and Spokane. The mountains and pine trees are beautiful, so beautiful. Very beautiful …

Our trip out here did not cost so very much and the tires held up pretty good. Drove about 1,800 to 2,000 miles with only 2 flat tires! One was up in the mountains at night but we got it changed – great fun really! Ellen Jean and I have had some swell times together out here. Too bad it has to change … well, for a while I guess it will. But perhaps it will end soon …

At Geiger Field, Carl's commanding officer had looked at this gregarious young man and the others assembled before him and knew that he was going to take away their youth forever. However, it was his job to teach them what it meant to be an officer, and what they had to prepare for in the conflict ahead. The CO was good at his job, and a good soldier, and he taught them well. Under his CO's tutelage, Carl began to mature from a carefree youth to a man. He also began to realize just what the future might hold for him as the Army Air Corps training program prepared him for the task ahead … prepared him to go to war.

October 10, 1942
Dear Folks
I thought I had better drop you folks a line. I am flying tonight which means I should be sleeping but I'm not tired so I will write all I can, and hope that I can mail this to you.

After arriving at Salt Lake City I received orders to report here, so here I am. This field isn't bad. Only thing is us new officers can't seem to find out what our duties are. Things are rather mixed up at the present. But it looks like next week perhaps we shall get things ironed out – I hope …

Since I am on duty 24 hours per day, they require us to live on the post. All the married officers are required to do this. But I got Ellen Jean an "all hours" pass to visit me on the post. So she has been driving out every evening from town and spending the evenings with me at "The Club." She has a nice place to stay in town I guess. It does not cost much.

Chances are that I will have Ellen Jean move in with you folks ... she can fix up the basement room and live there. Chances are that she will get work while I am in England. I will not go before Christmas, but I will be in stations where Ellen Jean will not be able to follow so I will send her and the car back to you folks. I prefer it that way.

It is a shame to have to write such stuff but our commanding officer told us that this is best. So I think perhaps Massey's wife will drive back with Ellen Jean at the end of this month or next month. Our commanding officer said that we should have everything ready to move out in short notice because we might have to pull out at any time. You know I have been selected to be on a combat crew already. I might have to go soon to fill up a crew, you know, "fill-in." Then again, I might be in the United States until February, one never knows.

Also our officer said we will be flying the world's safest airplane. With half decent luck we should come back OK. One never knows. But these B-17 Flying Fortresses are pretty good planes. There are 5 gunners aboard and they should be able to do me some good. You seldom read or hear about a B-17 ever getting shot down, so perhaps I am in luck!

Carl's enthusiasm about the Boeing B-17 "Flying Fortress" was not completely misplaced. The B-17 became noted for its ability to absorb horrific battle damage, still reach its target and bring its crew home safely. Stories abound of B-17s returning to base with tails having been destroyed, with only a single engine functioning or even with large portions of wings or nose having been damaged by flak.

However, Carl was also painfully aware of the odds he and the other

men of the Eighth Air Force faced. His CO had made that perfectly clear. So when his CO advised that the men get their affairs in order before they were deployed, Carl followed through.

October 10, 1942 (cont.)
One of these days soon you will receive an envelope marked "Will." This you must put away and do not open it or read it until after I am reported dead ... even then you should wait at least 1 month. But when you do open it I want you, every one of you, to follow it to the letter.

There will be 3 copies made, exactly alike. One will go to you folks, one to Ellen Jean and the other will be in my luggage. So when they ship my luggage home you will find one there.

Of course I am not planning on you folks ever opening my wills or having to read them, but one never knows does one? Might slip in the bathtub ... or sit on a tack.

November 2, 1942
I am writing this at the club. I can look out one of the windows down

toward the main gate. I am looking for Ellen Jean, she should be here in the next ½ hour, about 2:30 I guess. I don't have any insurance on the car so they might not let her bring it on the post. But she has every day so far. It's nice they let her come out every day.

I imagine you folks miss my daily letter but I don't have much time. I will continue to write as often as possible. I should like to hear from you folks so if you write airmail I might be able to get a few letters from you folks yet. I hope so …

Out here they are playing a new piece of music called, "White Christmas." It is rather pretty. Tell Gloria to learn it and play it. The piece has such a pretty melody. In fact the melody makes me want to pack up the car and start home, bet I would be there before this letter gets there and that's pretty fast!

It has been hazy out here, cool and cloudy weather. But it is enjoyable and refreshing. Wish you could make a trip out here to see me but that is out.
I might go to Topeka. If I do I will "buzz" Hutchinson so look for me. Look for the biggest plane you have ever seen to go over town in the next 20 or 40 days. Perhaps I will get to stop for a few hours. I will do my best to stop if I can. Tell Gloria to write if she has time. Also tell her to get all the schooling she can. I will write you later.

As Ever,
Carl

The change was coming soon.

1943

As the year swung into 1943, Carl and Ellen Jean found themselves in Blythe, California where Carl would undergo further flight training. Blythe was on the border between Arizona and California, in the desert, and "hotter than hell." It was here they would learn how to be bomber pilots. Carl found himself a 1st pilot, with a crew assigned to him for the first time. It was another one of those moments that changed things forever. The crew that would become such an integral

part of his life consisted of:

Bob Ward – co pilot
George Fisher – top gunner
Jack Jillson – waist gunner
Marty Stachiowiak – waist gunner
Ray Ford – turret gunner
Gayther Crowther – radioman
George Molnar – navigator
Tommy Kelly – tail gunner
Steve Gibson – bombardier

These were the men that would learn to depend on each other for their very lives. But the February day when they were first gathered, they were fresh-faced kids, except for Tommy Kelly an older guy who had been around the block a few times. The men had no real idea what they would face next. They still thought they were invincible.

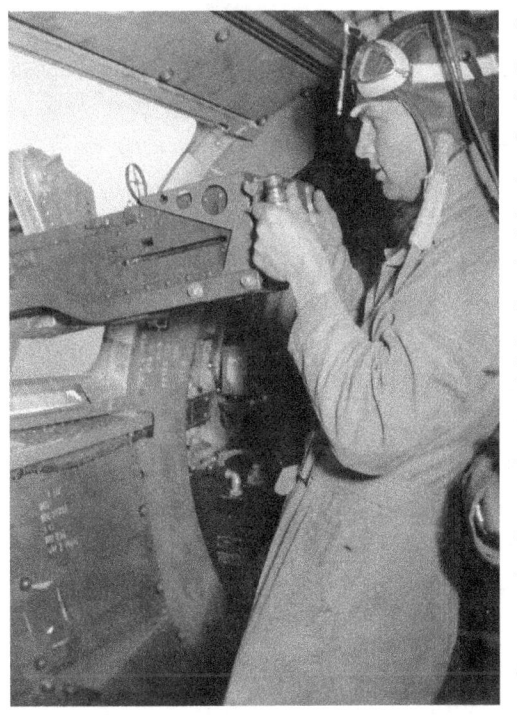

Carl's group was then ordered to the base dubbed "Rattlesnake" at Peyote, Texas. The base had earned this nickname because of the hundreds of rattlesnake dens unearthed in the construction of the base. The men flew in piloting the B-17's assigned to go to the base. The north wind was blowing across the barren west Texas plains and the runway at gale force. There were "Texas Cowboys" guarding all the gates. Sagebrush was the only vegetation around, growing up seven or eight feet tall. And yes, there were rattlesnakes. The base was aptly named. Carl remembered the look on Ellen Jean's face as she took in her temporary home, her nose wrinkled up in disgust. This was not going to be like the previous assignments. There were no beaches, no fancy hotels, no ballrooms to dance and laugh with the boys in like in California. There were no beautiful mountains with lovely streams to go fishing in like in Washington. Carl knew this was not what she wanted or what she was used to, but it wouldn't be forever. He hoped she would stick it out with him.

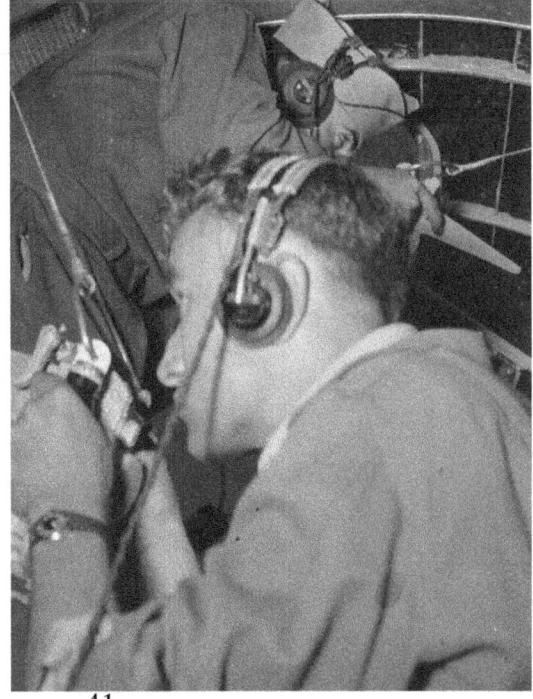

March 12, 1943

Dear Folks,
Just a few lines to let you know that I received in the morning mail 5 letters from you. One was dated January 11th, one was up to date. I was glad to get the pictures. Gloria looks very nice. As soon as I can I will let you know more about if you can make a trip down here. Things are all messed up here ... you know – "situation normal." ... Ellen Jean lives at Monnahans, Texas, which is 16 miles due east of here. She lives above the Lone Star Café. The car is parked out in front all the time. She and Lt. Alsop's wife went to Odessa, Texas and bought a new coat and hat, so they could get them before the clothing rationing goes into effect. You had better do the same. Also Ellen Jean is wearing her hair differently and it looks really swell! I get to see Ellen Jean about every 3 days as I am terribly busy.

Carl knew Ellen Jean hated that little town and the tacky apartment above the greasy spoon. She was lonely and bored silly. Carl was never home ... he spent most of his time in an airplane. Ellen Jean had nothing to do but stare at the walls or listen to the radio tell of the war. She didn't want to think about the war. She didn't want to think about what would happen when Carl got sent overseas. She hated this war! Ellen Jean would have much rather spent her time dancing in San Francisco with all those lovely boys from Buffalo ...

One positive thing that happened in Peyote was that Jack Jillson and his new bride became friendly with Ellen Jean and Carl. The two couples enjoyed socializing with each other, even though Carl was an officer and Jack was an enlisted man. They even took one delightful trip together to New Mexico in Carl's 1937 Chevy Coupe. Here they explored Carlsbad Caverns together, laughing and telling jokes, as young and carefree as 20-year-olds should be.

It was the last bit of fun any of them would have for some time to come.

March 15, 1943

Dear Folks,

Been several days since I have received any mail from you, so I thought I had better write. I have been real busy, flying and all. Today I found out that in the 9 days I have been here I have flown 52 hours. That's a lot of flying and I am not just a kidding!

I have been flying formations day and night, also bombing from 20,000 feet. Today we (three of us pilots) flew our ships over the gunnery range at 200 miles per hour in formation at 150 feet, all guns firing. (There are 11 guns on my ship that can shoot at once!) So with all three ships that makes 33 guns, which can shoot, each gun at 6,000 shots per minute, or all three ships put out 33,000 shots per

minute.

I have a couple of boys on my crew that can really shoot. The others are fair shots.

Last night I almost had an accident. I landed with a flat tail wheel (with 10 men on board). I really tore the tail wheel up but we made a safe landing.

The other day the top turret man shot over my head, over the cockpit at the target. Bang! All the windows broke and the guns were shooting 6 inches from my ears. Boy was I deaf and frightened! We were about 75 feet off of the ground doing 200 miles per hour!

We are having rather nice-mild weather here, but not as nice as California. I hope you get to come here soon, but I don't know when …

Carl and the men frequently would fly "tanker trips" from Peyote to Tucson, Arizona to get the 100-octane gasoline needed at the base. Over the dry mountains Carl would look down and see the wreckage of downed planes from practice missions that had gone awry. On one such trip back from Tucson, he watched in horror as a B-24 smashed into the ground north of El Paso Texas. There were no survivors. These experiences left Carl sober, thinking that these planes were really not to be messed around with. He would see worse before the year was out.

April 27, 1943

Dear Folks,
Here I am with my crew, out over the Gulf of Mexico, out of sight of land. It will be three hours before we do see land again. We are flying at 12,000 feet. We left the shore of Florida about 30 minutes ago. We all have on our "Mae West's". (These are the regular yellow Army life preservers.) We have had a real trip of this. This morning we flew a training mission from New Orleans to Florida where we were "attacked" by 12 persistent ships. They really put on a show. They came in like they really meant business. They really opened up and came through our formation. Now we are on our way back home. We have been in the air 6-1/2 hours so far today. We will get in about 8 hours of flying time. The navigator says it will take 2 more hours to get home, so we will not have much gas I betcha. We took our lunch along. I had a sandwich and an orange.

Not much else to write. The third phase of training is over so I may go to Salina soon.

Oh, in case you were wondering, I have turned on the automatic pilot so I can write this. It relieves me from piloting the plane, it does OK."

May 1, 1943

… Well, our work is about done here at Peyote. Chances are that I will take my crew to Salina soon. Be on the look out for me! If you hear a plane flying over low, changing up the engine sound, that might be me!!!!! Expect us soon …

It was early in May of 1943 when Carl and his crew got their orders. All the training and practicing was over. Ellen Jean would be packed up and taken home to live in the basement of his parent's house while he was away. They had talked about it and he had thought about this moment so often, and now it was here. It was time to join the war for real.

Deep inside, Carl knew he was prepared, and he felt confident that he had what it took. There was that long line of Fyler military blood flowing through his veins. He knew he had been born for this moment.

Carl and Ellen Jean hastily threw their belongings in the Chevy and drove through the night to get to Hutchinson, Kansas. It was the first time back home since he had joined the service, and he had been very homesick. His family had always been close, and Carl had never been far away from home. It felt good to be with them again. Sadly, it was a brief reunion.

The night before he was scheduled to leave for Europe, Carl and Ellen Jean sat up talking and holding each other way into the early morning hours. She had snuggled close and her kisses were full of passion. He would never forget how she wrapped her arms around him and cried, begging him to do anything but leave her here. Carl then told her something that later he realized was probably a turning point in the relationship. He tried to explain to her that an officer's duty often carried him away from those he loved. His commanding officer had taught them this. It was country first, then family and home, because any country that couldn't protect family and home wasn't much of one. Carl had understood what the CO had told him. If Ellen Jean did not come to understand that it was this love for his country and for fellow humans superseded all else, she would never really understand him. He loved Ellen Jean deeply, but he loved his God and his country more. Carl tried to convince her, to make her understand the rightness of his words. He believed those words, he had made them his own, but it was breaking his heart to have to tell it to Ellen Jean, when at that moment he felt something so different …

The next morning Carl and John, who would drive the Chevy back to Hutchinson, took off to Salina, Kansas, leaving Ellen Jean to feel like she had been unceremoniously dumped into the dungeon basement of the Fyler house. The moment she had been dreading had arrived. Her handsome, dark-haired flyboy was going into harm's way. Unreasonably somehow she felt as if he were doing that just to spite her. Her future was in his hands. She watched as the two men pulled out of the driveway and headed down the road as Mother Fyler waved like a fool, long after the car had disappeared into the dust. A sense of dread came to sit like a rock in the pit of her stomach. The life she had dreamed of was driving down that road.

It took Carl and John a little more than an hour to drive to Salina, where there was a huge air force base named after the blue hills of grass that surrounded it … The Smoky Hills Air Force Base. It was at this base that the B-17s were equipped with the weaponry they would need to fight a war. The locationof the base in the relatively flat prairie lands of Kansas made it the perfect place to put in long concrete runways fit for the big, heavy planes. It later became a Strategic Air Command base. It was renamed Schilling Air Force Base in 1948 in honor of Colonel David Schilling who was a fighter pilot with 23 kills against the German Luftwaffe. But for now, Carl was tickled pink that the base was so close to home. He had been saying all along he wanted to surprise the folks back in Spearville, and now he was going to get his chance.

As Carl pulled up to the main building at the base, he was greeted with the glorious vision of a shiny new B-17F, complete with ball turret and the new paddle bladed propellers. Carl couldn't wait. He had been scheming in his mind about this moment ever since he went to flight school. He and his crew scrambled into the beautiful new bird and took her out for the test ride of her life. He headed straight out to western Kansas, with the clear blue skies and white clouds surrounding the plane. He made a beeline to Hodgeman County where his Uncle Joe Dvorak's ranch was located. As he buzzed over the roof of the house, he changed the prop pitch on all four propellers, which added more decibels to the loud rumble the B-17 made normally, shaking the house and the ground for miles around. Uncle Joe ran out of the house. Aunt Lyda, who was out hanging up laundry, dropped her basket, then realizing it was friend not foe, grabbed a pillow case and began waving it joyously at her nephew as he returned her greeting from the cockpit. Then Carl flew to Spearville. He directed the plane down the center of Main Street. As he approached the steeple of the Catholic Church he did a maneuver called a chandelle up over the steeple. Aunt Lyda must have phoned ahead, because people ran out into Main Street waving towels, then on to Hutchinson to give his parents a show too. Carl threw back his head and laughed in joy. He felt young and free, and he so loved to fly. For a while that afternoon the thrill of flight overtook any concerns about heading off to war.

The joy ride over, they turned and flew back to Salina, ready to go to Bangor, Maine, and then across the sea to England. They left Salina on May 29, 1943. As they flew over Gary, Indiana, it occurred to Carl that they should have some radio problems which would require them to make a landing at Selfridge Field in Detroit, Michigan, where it just so happened his navigator's family lived. Carl allowed the young man to phone home. Miraculously the radio problem had fixed itself when they returned to the plane, and soon they were on the way again.

At the Bangor base Carl and his crew loaded up on everything they thought they would need overseas. Carl, always one for sweets, bought a large carton of Hershey's candy bars. You never knew what to expect, and Carl didn't want to neglect his sweet tooth. The ground crew loaded up large cases of cigarettes for the men to deliver at Goose Bay Air Base in Labrador along the shores of Canada.

The men and their aircraft crossed the St. Lawrence waterways and headed to the north. Roads and houses grew smaller and smaller and disappeared as the plane gained altitude. Navigation became questionable over the sparse area, and Carl found himself a bit nervous. At last they found Goose Bay. When Carl brought the plane down at the base, it was May 31, 1943.

This was the first time Carl had ever seen the Atlantic Ocean. It was also the first time for his navigator. But they were young and certain of their own longevity and they had their orders, so they would fly across the great ocean. It was June 1, 1943, a bright cloudless morning, when the heavily laden B-17F headed across those cold waters, heading east for Europe. The radios did not work, the compass was erratic, but the sun was out and so they decided to shoot the sun for their course.

There was no way the B-17 could make it across the Atlantic without refueling and the feat of mid-air refueling was still in the future. So the crew touched down in Greenland, very nearly out of gas.

The crew was exhausted from this long flight, and so they slept. The windows of the boarding house had heavy black drapes over them to block out the midnight sun, which was so bright a person could read by it at night if the curtains were left open. Carl had no desire to read. He closed the drapes and slept for nearly two days.

On June 3, the crew took off for Scotland. The plane lifted and climbed to 11,000 feet. Carl headed to the southeast on course. When he thought he was near land, he lowered the aircraft to 200 feet through a dark and cloudy night. He could not see the ground. He kept thinking about all the things he had heard and read about the hills of Scotland. He had always wanted to see those hills someday, but he did not want to be introduced to them by slamming an airplane into them. He tried one last time, but still there was no visibility. At that point he gave up and headed toward Ireland. Once he had located where the plane's position was, he turned due east and crossed the Irish Sea. There were English warships in the water beneath the plane. Carl sincerely hoped those sailors were thinking, "There goes another bloody Yank!" and would not shoot at them! Fortunately the ships did not shoot, and they headed up for Prestwick, Scotland and landed on the wet grass.

The next flight took Carl and his crew to Burtonwood Air Depot in Liverpool, England. The B-17 would stay here, but Carl and his men would move on. Next they boarded a train headed south to Watford near London. At Watford they took another train to RAF Bovington. There they attended more combat training.

Carl took one day off and ventured into London on his own. The underground train he took landed him in Piccadilly Station. He walked around London, saw the sights and ate a meal at the Rainbow Club, which was a Red Cross Club for servicemen. He was amazed to learn that the British drink their soda pop and their beer warm. Carl had learned that if he just retraced his steps, he never got lost, so at the end of the day he retraced his steps back to Piccadilly and headed back to the base.

While he was at this base he saw the crew of the famous B-17, Memphis Belle, receive her reward from the King and Queen for completing 25 missions. He was to later learn that the first B-17 to fly 25 missions was really the "Hell's Angels" from the 303rd Heavy Bomb group, but they couldn't get that plane ready in time for the reporters.

After this interlude, Carl and his buddies got on the train headed for Molesworth Air Base, the home of the very same 303rd Heavy Bomb Group.

"Molesworth took its name from a nearby English village. It was situated about 70 miles north of London in the Midlands region known as East Anglia. East Anglia was chosen because it had considerable open space and level terrain and it was relatively close to mainland Europe, thus shortening flights and allowing for greater bomb loads. It was a self-contained base, with all the

support facilities and personnel needed to service the 303rd's four squadrons – the 358th, 359th, 360th and the 427th. The base also served as headquarters for the 8th Air Force's 41st Combat Wing, comprising the 303rd, the 379th Bomb Group located four miles to the south, and the 384th which was located eight miles to the west of Molesworth. From the air, the base could be easily recognized by its triangle of three runways. The field's 7,000-foot-long main runway ran east and west. It was intersected at its end by a smaller north-south runway. A third runway that aligned northwest to southeast formed the third leg of the triangle. Ringing this triangle were many other taxiways that led off to the heavy bomber hardstands. At the center of this spider web of runways stood a large technical site where the planes were serviced and repaired. The site also contained the control tower, a huge J-type aircraft hanger, two smaller hangers, and a complex of other buildings including the headquarters building for the 41st Wing, the Group Headquarters, Base Facility Operations offices, enlisted and officer's mess halls, and the buildings and barracks that belonged to the men of the Squadrons." (2)

Carl and crew found their new home to be a steel Nissan hut. It was not fancy and it was not particularly warm, but the little hut would become a safe haven from the horror they were about to enter.

Life was OK at Molesworth. The air was cold and damp there. Carl remembered always feeling chilled to the bone there. It would take a couple of hot Kansas summers for him to feel really warm again! The cold men in the hut were only allowed one shovelful of coal dust to burn that lasted about an hour. George Fisher finally got tired of being constantly cold, so he made a furnace out of an oil drum. He placed the drum on a raised platform outside of the barrack and rigged it so that airplane fuel dripped into a chamber to be burned. This proved to be a very effective furnace. It kept the barracks nice and warm until a Major who was a stickler for the rules came along and ripped the furnace out.

The men lived an emotional roller coaster sort of existence. When they flew, it was as if they were in another world devoid of anything other than the primary will to live and to return to base. These days were interspersed with calm days on the ground. This was disorienting and a very different experience than the constant stress of battle and living in the field as encountered by troops on the ground.

Carl would remember those days and the battle missions he flew in vivid, gory color details, all the rest of his life. They lived inside of him and replayed in his head like a movie set to replay, over and over again. Carl's crew lived those days of horror together in the air. They lived or died in concert in the sky. Each one's life was completely dependent on the actions of the others. Carl grew closer to those nine men, and their replacements, than any family tie he had ever had. For most, these bonds would last for the rest of their lives.

"Dr. Malcom C. Grow, the Eighth Air Force's chief surgeon, later told Intelligence Investigators, "These men are not interested in democracy or freedom; they are interested in their team. The teams are the closest-knit things that you have ever seen." What kept them going was their desire to help the team. They would never want to let the other men down." (1)

They were joined together in spirit as surely as they were by the hose lines and wires and intercoms in the planes. They would fight through their fears for each other.

The truth was there was plenty about which to be fearful.

"By October of 1943, fewer than one out of four Eighth Air Force crew members would live to complete their tour of duty. By

the end of the war, the Eighth Air Force would have more fatal casualties: 26,000, than the entire United States Marine Corps. 77 percent of those Americans who flew against the Reich before D-Day would not return home to their loved ones alive. " (1)

On the day of the mission, the crews were called out of bed at 3 or 4 a.m. After preparing for the day they would head to the mess hall for breakfast. On non-mission days they got powdered eggs but on mission days they got fresh eggs, a good breakfast. They would need the energy for the long day ahead. Next the crew attended a briefing by the Commanding Officer. The men would be informed as to what to expect on the mission; targets, flak predictions, weather, and information that might be pertinent to the success of the mission.

Meanwhile, the planes were being made ready for the mission as well. Armaments experts hauled wooden crates stacked with belts of .50 caliber shells into the planes, placing a box at each gunner's station. They also inspected the guns and the power operated gun turrets, making sure everything was in working order. When these men had finished their work, the ground mechanics – three men to a plane – took over, making sure that everything on the Fortress was in perfect order: engine, hydraulics, brakes, tires, electronics, and oxygen systems. Each one of these duties was crucial to the safety of the men in the air. It was a life or death operation.
After the briefing the crew would be taken by Jeep to the airfield. There they would wait until they were called. If they had to wait it was usually due to weather. They would send up a flare. If the flare was green, it was a go; the mission was on. If it was red, it meant the mission was delayed or cancelled.

This was in some ways the hardest part of the mission, the waiting on the airfield. The airmen had a saying; "You die on the runway, not after you are hit." This is when the nerves hit. Once in the air, there was a job to do. Nerves could be funneled into action. It was waiting for the job to begin that was killer. Many times the pilots would have to talk the men down on the field. The pilot functioned like the captain of a team. The men would gather around the pilot as he spoke words to shore them up for their duty. No fancy speech by any General or President would reassure the men more than the words of their pilot. Carl had always been a leader, but as he saw the way his crew responded to his words, he began to understand the responsibility that lay on his shoulders. He drew from deep within him, and soon began to grow from a youth into a man that could inspire the other men to follow him to hell and back. This was a crucial component to the missions. The crews that made it back were the ones who had a pilot who could lead them through it all and back again.

And so at last the flare would fly. If the flare went green the engines on the planes would all fire up at once in a great roar. The engines were 1200HP and they used 50 gallons of fuel per engine per hour. The total weight of a loaded B-17 was 30 tons. Because they were so heavy the planes needed a lot of runway to get off the ground. The runways at Molesworth were barely long enough. If a plane didn't get high enough and went off the end of the runway and hit a tree, there would be a huge explosion and fireball. Approximately 400 planes and 4,000 men were lost in this way.

After the Fortresses were airborne they would circle the field to get to altitude, then get in formation. They flew in formation to protect themselves from the enemy gunfire. If the enemy planes came at them from straight ahead, which they usually did, the rate of closure was two seconds, so they only had two seconds to fire and hit the planes before they were on them. Then they would reassemble as they could and move on to the target.

In his personal diary, Carl would describe his missions in detail:

Mission # 1   7-1-43
Turned back at the coast due to bad engine

Mission # 2   7-4-43 Le Mans France
Today was LeMans Airfield. July 4th was a good day to start combat! It was a bright clear day. We crossed into France northwest of Paris. I was flying the number 2 position on the lead plane. A single German FW190 fighter came at us about 11:00 level. The navigator got off a good burst of .50s. The fighter carried on, not firing a single shot. It

looked like he wanted to ram us. I hauled our plane to one side and missed the fighter. A B-17 behind us went down. I counted only 5 chutes, half of the 10-man crew. We bombed the target and returned to base. I had mission #1 under my belt and it felt good.

Mission # 3   7-10-43 Abbeville, France
Abbeville Air Base was just across the English Channel into France. Stationed there were the German's best fighters, known as the "Abbeville Kids." We had no fighter escort again. When the enemy fighters would shoot at us from head on I would pull my bird up 40-50-feet, and in the next attack I would drop down 40-50-feet. This way the shells would go over or under head. The navigator gave me hell for this as he too could see the shells coming. We bombed the target and returned to base safely.

I had a surprise in store for me upon return from this raid … a 48-hour pass in London. I rode a GI truck to Bedford and caught the train into London's St. Pancreas RR Station. I saw the sights of the city and stayed the night at the Red Crown "Reindeer" Club for officers. It wasn't all fun and games in London though. There was an air raid that night. I just stayed in bed in total darkness with the sheets up around my ears because I did not know where the air-raid shelters were.

When I got back to the base I went to quarters and found several of my men having a chicken fry. A steel helmet was on the heating stove filled with butter to cook the chickens in. Seven chickens had paid the price and several loaves of English bread. This was a real feast! There was much laughing and singing and carrying on that night.

Mission #4   7-17-43   Hanover Germany
Hanover was 50 miles into Germany. Due to the number of B-17s aborting and the dense undercast, we did not bomb the target, but enemy fighters came up anyway. There were Me109s and FW-190s. Our formation was quite bad. At one point I saw a tail gunner on another plane jump out, but his chute did not open. He fell into the cold North Sea. His ship was flying on only two engines, but with the skill of her pilots she and the rest of the crew made it back to England.

After the indiscriminate bombing of London the Luftwaffe was conducting, and a vicious attack on Coventry, the USAAF decided to retaliate. The Allies decided to bomb the "humane" way, which meant warning the civilian populations. One day we got into our combat togs, and went out to the aircraft and watched while wooden crates loaded with pamphlets went into the bomb bays of our B-17s. The pamphlets were red white, and blue, with one side in English and the other in German, telling the people they should evacuate Hamburg because The RAF and USAAF would be back soon to bomb the city. Then we fought our way to Hamburg, risking our lives to deliver the warning. What we really did was prepare the Luftwaffe for our return.

Mission #5   7-24-43   Heroya, Norway

Heroya was where Hitler's heavy water plant was located. Germany was working on building an atomic bomb. It was clear that day and so we flew over the North Sea at only 10,000 feet. We were told that if we went into the frigid waters below, death by hypothermia would come in 45 seconds. As I approached Norway I thought its mountains and fjords resembled Greenland. The target plant was situated on a peninsula. The two bomber groups ahead of us bombed the target and the results looked good. We came next. On the bomb run I could see the battery of seven AA flak guns on the ground firing at us. Their barrels flashed red, and then three seconds later shells would explode near us. Some were like black sand that hit the windshield. One .88-millimeter shell exploded between the #2 engine and myself. I ducked my head under the panel. I was relieved when the shell did no damage, as it exploded in a "Y" pattern. Some metal fragments went up, and some went down, but none went sideways. That burst was a little too close for comfort! Our right wing was substantially damaged by the flak.

We were in the air 8 hours on that mission, flying some 1,300 miles. It was one of the longest missions I flew, and one of many without fighter escort.

Mission # 6   7-25-43   Hamburg Germany

It was a bright clear day and I could see for 50 miles. The tempera-

ture at our altitude of 30,000 feet was anywhere from -55 to -60 degrees C. The Germans had taken our paper warnings seriously and the flak was quite intense as we approached Hamburg. There was so much flak I almost felt like I could step out of the plane and walk on it. I watched a friend's plane get hit just ahead of us. The men fell out of the plane and went down ahead of it. On another plane, several men passed out from lack of oxygen. This was a common problem in the B-17s. Often the saliva and condensation from our breath would freeze at such cold temperatures, blocking the air lines on our oxygen masks. A person would not realize that the mask or tubing was blocked, and die from lack of oxygen before they even realized it. Tail gunners had particular problems with this. These men survived, but they both had frostbite. Another man's eyelids froze shut.

Sometimes I would see bursts of flak directly in my intended path. One puff, then another, then 3. I was sure the next would explode right under my seat, but in a few seconds the tail gunner exclaimed, in very colorful language, "My God that was close back here." By luck our airspeed was just right to miss the flak bursts

On the final bomb run the flak was bad. Ahead of us I saw a vertical square box of solid black flak. It was a horrible sight. I swallowed my fear and we flew into it. To this day I wonder how we got the courage to fly into that aerial hell, but we flew through it without getting hit. We dropped our bombs, making a turn after "bombs away." I looked back and saw a column of fire rise up into the sky, 2,000 feet high. Later I was to learn that this city was also a night bombing target for the RAF. After those bombing raids that city was turned into a mass of fire from all the incendiary bombs dropped there. Firestorms raged throughout the city and 40,000 civilians died. Flight time on this trip was six and a half hours.

Mission # 7   7-27-43   Kassel Germany.
We hit bad weather right after takeoff. With a full bomb load, full fuel and full crew, I struggled to climb through the dark clouds to 30,000 feet. I called back and asked the crew to look in all directions for any oncoming aircraft and to scream at me which way to go to avoid a collision because I was flying blind. Three times the bird stalled

and got away from me. Three times I recovered it. At last we broke through the overcast. Planes were popping out into the sun everywhere.

We circled and formed up. We started for Kassel, crossed the North Sea and entered Germany, but the weather prevented us from finding our target. On our way home we dumped our bombs into the North Sea. We didn't want to try to land with the British rubber/gas types of bombs we were carrying that day. After our return we learned that 5 of our aircraft were lost in collisions while climbing through the bad weather. In those planes only one crew man had survived, because he had unstrapped his seat belt and pulled his ripcord.

Mission #8 7-28-43 Kiel Germany

Our target was Kiel Navy base on the east coast of Germany. Things went routinely as we dressed, ate, were briefed, boarded, started up, took off, formed up, and flew over the North Sea, crossing the German occupied coast. Then we were attacked by German fighters. The weather over the target was poor. We were at 21,000 feet and the flak was accurate. We took a good hit in the right wing. Both right engines quit after losing our fuel through the many holes. We dropped down to the deck. I rolled in all the trim we had. My co-pilot, Bob Ward and I pushed hard on the left rudder, really standing on it and we started for home. We flew almost sideways for 500 miles across the North Sea at 100 feet. It looked bad. We stayed at it, still pushing hard on the left rudder pedals. We kept the plane banked into the left wing with the two good engines. Off the coast of Holland, a Ju-88 twin Stuka came up after us. We were so low and in such a pronounced skid, he could not hit us. Our tail gunner, S/Sgt Kelly got him.

As we came up on the east coast of England, we were in luck as the land sloped into the sea and there were no cliffs. I saw a big black-topped emergency landing strip. We headed for it. Our flight engineer, T/Sgt Bill Addison checked the landing gear and tires as best he could. We continued our skidding until over the runway, cut the throttles, straightened out as best we could and let her down. The zing of the tires was a wonderful sound. We had made it. We were so glad to be alive, I don't even recall how we got back to base.

In a Vmail home on this date, Carl wrote:
Well I wonder what you are doing back home right now. Just think it is evening here and time for bed, back home it is only noon and you are probably ready for dinner. Kinda hard to visualize the time difference and all …

There is no indication of the things Carl had seen or the fears he had faced. But they are there.

Mission # 9   8-12-43   Geisenkirchen Germany, Rurh Valley.
On August 12th we were to hit the synthetic oil plant at Gelsenkirchen Germany. The Germans had a method of converting oil into benzene for the war machine. At briefing we were told that we would have to fly south down to the Ruhr Valley to the target, and that over 1,200 flak guns lined this 60 mile stretch. I saw four types of flak that day: grey, black, brown and rose colored. There were also about 250 German fighters. Seven of our B-17s just exploded. Some went down in a white puff – then nothing. At other times I would see a puff, then four smoking engines but no other falling pieces. Some birds just slid out of formation and went down. Often we would see only 2 chutes opening as the men jumped, or tried to.

The B-17 in front of us surprised me when it "snap rolled" right in formation. Then he entered a spin and went down. I stood up in the cockpit to try to see if anyone got out. For 10,000 feet it fell; there were no chutes. My guess is that the pilot must have been hit to make it snap roll like that. The G forces must have prevented the crew from bailing out.

The enemy fighter attacks were vicious that day, as was the cold at that altitude. We lost 25 B-17s on that mission.

Clark Gable flew with us on this mission. He was the top turret gunner with Capt. Calhoun's group. Gable was not the only celebrity to fly with us. Correspondent Walter Cronkite also flew on some missions with our Heavy Bomber Group.

It may have been this mission when I first saw German air-to-air rockets. A fighter off to my left fired two balls of orange at our B-17. They rolled across the sky at us. They did not seem very fast. After landing again at Molesworth I found two round holes about 17 inches across in each side of the fuselage, just ahead of the ball turret and radio bulkhead. The holes were almost like 2 new windows! I reported these balls of fire to the Intelligence officers at debriefing. They did not believe me. It wasn't until later they realized the Germans were indeed firing rockets at us.

A v-mail home after this mission read:

Dear Folks,
Haven't received any mail from you for a number of days. In fact, none since the middle of last week. Been a long time.

Steve was just now kidding that we would be home in time for Thanksgiving, turkey dinner and all. George thinks Christmas. Myself, I think next 4th of July.

Today is Friday the 13th. Glad I don't have to work today like I did yesterday. I guess I am a bit superstitious.

Is it still pretty hot back there yet? I wish I were there and could get a suntan or go swimming again. That is all for now.

As always, Carl

Carl and his companions were awash in homesickness and a growing fatigue by this time. They were dreaming about Thanksgiving and Christmas, and longing for swimming and suntans. Carl wrote to his family about work, as if he were heading off to an office each day. His parents and Ellen Jean could not even imagine what he had seen and done. Even Carl couldn't put it into words. But there were more missions to complete. After 25 missions, he could go home. This is what he and his crew lived for. When the war first began, there was no magic number of missions. However, the commanders soon learned that the crew could not fight under such horrific conditions without some end in sight, some light at the end of the tunnel. And so it was determined that after a man flew 25 missions, he would either be sent home or reassigned to another type of job somewhere else in the field. However, the sobering fact was that it was deemed statistically impossible for any full crew to reach their 25th mission. Despite this, as the war ground on, the number of available men and planes began to plummet, causing the magic number to be pushed up to 30, then 35.

The men of Carl's crew began to count the numbers ...

Mission # 10   8-16-43   Amiens France
Our target was the Pouix Air Base at Amiens France. The weather was good and we dropped 24 100 lb. bombs right on target.

While Carl and the 303rd HBG were pounding away at their targets, General Arnold was growing impatient with the progress of the European air war.

"It was later observed that the operation was the outgrowth of a desire to find an easy way of ending the war. There were three main targets of importance to making a quick end to Germany's ability to make war: oil production plants, ball bearing production plants, and aircraft plants. It was decided that it was better to cause massive destruction in a few really essential elements of the German war machine than to cause a small degree of destruction in many parts of the machine. The Germans had already proved that they could quickly repair small amounts of damage. The top minds decided that they must inflict very heavy damage when they did hit." (1)

"It was obvious that anti-friction bearings played a vital role in any industrial economy, but 1940s-era German machinery was believed to be more dependent on ball bearings than most. It was estimated, for example, that the German aviation industry consumed an average of 2.4 million bearings per month. The fact that bearing construction was concentrated in just a few plants, with Schweinfurt accounting for more than 40 percent of produc-

tion, made the ball bearing industry in general, and Schweinfurt in particular, an obvious target. Making Schweinfurt even more attractive was its small size, which would make it easy for bombardiers to locate and hit the bearing plants – a factor that also made it a poor target for the RAF night bombers. German planners had belatedly realized the vulnerability of the bearing plants and began making plans to disperse them, but to do so would take time as well as disrupt production of the precious bearings."
—(Historynet.com)

Carl later wrote about his experience of this important mission:

Mission # 11   8-17-43   Schweinfurt Germany

This was the first Schweinfurt mission to the German ball bearing plant. The Officer of the Day got us up at 2:00 AM. We struggled into our clothes and long johns and went down to the briefing. The Intelligence Officer uncovered the map of Europe. The red yarn seemed to go across the world, deep into Germany. The Intelligence Officer said, "400 fighters will hit you on the way in with 1,200 big guns. 88s and 105s. The 400 fighters will refuel and hit you again on the way out. ... This did not sound good. The Group Commander stood up and said, "Men, the war will be over in 3 months if you hit the targets today! Bow your necks and get it done!" I was to fly an old beat-up B-17 F named "Red Ass" with an old type of oxygen system. With this system, when you breathed in the frozen slobber it went into your lungs as ice crystals.

The target was so important that a composite group was made up of spare planes and crews. I was flying with a mixed bunch from other bases. My former C.O. was to lead, Colonel (now a Major General) Lew Lyle. I was in the 2nd element of the lower squadron on the right side. We went out to where the big bird was parked. She was a dirty olive drab color with some black smoke and oils streaks on her.

England was socked in with a heavy fog. The gunners placed their gun barrels in the .50 caliber sheathes, checked the oxygen masks and gloves, goggles, electric suits and steel infantry helmets, as we did not yet have flak suits.

Everyone had a case of the nerves. Frequent "piss calls" were needed behind the planes. Others put on their oxygen masks and tried to clear their brains. Others could not get their cigarettes to their mouths because of nerves. We just waited and waited for the signal to start our engines. It was about noon when the fog lifted but the other division had already left for Regensburg, the target, and had to fly over the Alps to land in Africa. There we sat: we lost the support they would have given us with the enemy fighters.

The green flare came. We started those big-throated 1200 H.P. radial engines. They belched smoke, backfired and started, settling down to an even roar. Next we taxied out to our positions for take off. My turn came to take off. Pushing the throttles forward to get full boost, 8,000 feet down the runway we went and we were still on the ground. The air speed indicated 150 m.p.h. At the west end of the runway I pulled back on the yoke and the bird came off. Then there was the turn to the right to catch up with the rest of the squadron and form the composite group.

We climbed to an altitude of about 24,000 feet. It was minus 55 degrees C. The sun was out. It was a bright day. There was no cloud cover so we could see for miles over the continent. As we crossed the channel I had the men fire their guns and report if everything was operational. It was.

I had not been told that the men in the back felt they were not coming back so they stole 8 more cases of ammunition planning to go down fighting. They wanted to do it up right! With 3,000 gallons of 100-octane gasoline and 10 500lbs bombs and all the junk in the old bird, no wonder she was so slow getting off the runway!

As we approached the target, on my right I could see a row of German fighters lining up. They were all FW 190s. They'd pull around ahead of us and approach us head on, rolling over upside down and firing, going through the formations of the B-17s causing havoc. One came through at me. He rolled right side up and came over my right wing firing. My top turret gunner swung his guns to the right and fired point blank at the plane and got him. I could see the pilot's face as he went past me and down. There were 5 of these kinds of attacks – we lost the whole top squadron.

Planes were going down everywhere. Belts of .50 caliber ammunition came tumbling down from the sky as did gun barrels as frightened crews tried to lighten their load. The gasoline was going fast. The white chutes were our guys; the tan chutes were the enemy. At one point I counted about 100 chutes in the sky.

We dumped our load on the target, my crew shouting and cussing like mad. The plane shook from gunfire. Cordite, the gunpowder, was in the air and in my teeth. 23 of our B-17s went down on the way in to the target, still more on the way out. 280 planes went out that day, as many as 60 were lost.

The B17s with the wing tip tanks had already bombed Regensburg and were on their way to Africa. We started our "let down" and came off the oxygen. I fumbled for my sack of sandwiches. I ate all of the frozen Spam sandwiches. It had been 12 hours since I last ate. I was flying with one hand. We conserved our gasoline to get home. There were planes all over the sky, no formation left. We were down low as we crossed the English Channel. There was no gasoline left to transfer to the tanks. Off to my right I saw B-17s go down into the water, out of gas. I babied my bird along. At last we saw Molesworth and prepared to land.

The zip of tires hitting the concrete was a good sound. We could relax. I parked the bird. The squadron flight surgeon came out to our craft and gave each one of us a brown pottery English tea mug – full of American Bourbon.

I made my way to interrogation, made my report, went to the mess hall and ate, and then fell into bed exhausted. I slept a profound deep sleep that night.

Mission #12   8-19-43   Gilsen-Rijen Holland
The Intelligence Officer promised us this would be a "milk run." As we got to the target in the late afternoon, we quickly discovered he was wrong! We had to make 2 bomb runs. Our group lost 2 ships on the second run. I could see that one was on fire. I watched the crew jump.

As we neared the coast on the return trip, the enemy fighters fiercely attacked us. Two of my friend's crew were shot up and there were quite a few wounded. My bird had nose and wing damage from flak.

This was definitely not a milk run.

Mission # 13   8-23-43 North Sea mission
This mission was a rescue mission over the North Sea. We flew alone at 500 feet over the icy cold waters, looking for Canadian RAF crews that had been downed the night before after bombing in Germany. We carried yellow pillow-sized dinghys to drop if we saw them. We did not find any crewmen.

However, just 30 miles off of the German coast we did come upon a German Dornier 24, which was a three-engine seaplane, sitting on the water. We circled the bird at 500 feet like Indians circling a wagon train. My crew wanted to destroy it. Instead we shot its tail off and watched while its crew rowed away in their rubber raft. I saw no need to kill them. On the way back we were attacked by a Ju-88. We shot it down. Off the coast of Holland we downed another attacking Me-109.

Mission # 14   8-27-43   Watten France

We were assigned a 'secret target' in Watten France. It seemed very odd at the time. Perhaps we were bombing a V-1 buzz bomb launch site. I don't know. I just know the flak was very accurate. Two of our group went down over the target. A friend, Robert Cogswell, lost three engines and ended up gliding across the channel to a crash landing. He and his crew were okay.

I was heading the second element as we left the target, heading back to England. We were still over France when the ship in front of us took a direct hit in the cockpit. Chunks of flesh came back at us, splattering on our windshield. My copilot became ill. The stricken ship seemed to come to a complete stop. Since I was directly behind him, with wingmen on both sides, I could not stop to avoid a collision. I cut the throttles and fish tailed the bird, praying I'd miss the ship. Somehow it seemed to float over us and was gone.

All but one of our 20 ships were damaged by flak that day.

Mission # 15   9-3-43   Romily –Sur-Seine France

For this mission I had been assigned to a different aircraft. It was a YB-40. While it looked like a B-17, it carried no bombs, but plenty of ammunition. It had an extra turret. This turret was made in the field and held 4 British .303 machine guns. We passed Paris on the right, flying at 23,000 feet. It was cold in the cockpit that day. The enemy flak was accurate again. I saw four ships blow up in a single white puff. We were in the "tail end Charlie" position, also known as "Purple Heart corner" because so many ships were hit at that position. We lost one engine but continued to stay with the formation with full boost on the other three. Joe Bradshaw, my co-pilot, was just about to finish his 25th mission. As we neared the Molesworth airfield to land, he wanted me to do a "buzz job" so I let him "cut the grass," flying so low that the propellers would almost literally mow the grass. We flew in low, right in front of all the military brass who were watching from the tower. Joe was a lucky guy. He was through with the war!

Many will tell you the YB-40 never saw combat. Obviously they are wrong! After this mission I reported that the YB-40 was just too heavy and therefore too slow to be useful.

Mission # 16   9-4-43   Frankfurt Germany
V-mail:
We flew our 16th mission today. 9 more left. Hope our luck holds out …

Mission # 17   9-16-43   Stuttgart Germany
Our target was Stuttgart, deep into the heart of Germany. At altitude, visibility was very good. Way off to the south I could see the snow on the Swiss mountains. The trip was long. We used up a lot of gas. On the way back after hitting the targets our planes were all scattered – there were no real formations left. We were all trying to conserve fuel. To add to the concern, a 60 mph head wind was slowing us down. To increase our chances of making it back we were all throwing ammunition belts and guns overboard. One gun barrel was tossed overboard from another plane above us and hit a plane behind and below us between #1 and #2 engines, cutting the wing right off. The plane went down. Only 2 'chutes were seen. This was Lt. Benepe's plane. He was a close friend of mine.

I could still see the Swiss Alps and a big lake off to the left. I thought if we had to we might make a quick turn and head for the lake. Even with all the red panel lights showing low fuel, I continued west toward "home," getting gauges reading lower and lower all the time. Bombardier Steve Gibson was navigating as best he could.

Ahead of me, perhaps 100 feet higher, was 1st Lt. Bill Baker's B-17, at about 2 o'clock. Bill Baker was another good friend of mine. He was from our squadron. I could see that he was under attack by a twin-engine Me-110. The fighter was lobbing 20mm cannon shells into the tail, and I knew it would soon be a "kill." I screamed into the intercom "Can't someone help our B-17 over there?" Many of our barrels were burned out so that any shells fired would just pop at the end of the barrel and go nowhere. My right waist gunner, 35-year-old Martin Stachowiak jammed his glove into the mechanism and fired a few more rounds out of the flexible .50. From my seat I could see the tracers curve out ahead of us and into the Me-110 on the far wing, which folded into the two enemy crewmen in their cockpit. The Me-110 rolled once and went down. My pal and his crew were saved, at least for the moment. They were shot up pretty badly and could not stay in formation.

S/Sgt. Fielder was their flight engineer that day. Lt McLane was their navigator. S/Sgt. Norwood Borror, waist gunner went back to help S/Sgt. Charles M Bacon, the tail gunner, who had been hit in the shoulder. Borror brought the tail gunner up front to give him first aid. After that, Bacon sat on a wooden ammo box and fired a waist gun, destroying another ME-109 while the waist gunner also lay wounded on the floor. Baker would eventually get their Fort the rest of the way home. Bacon received the Silver Star for his efforts.

Meanwhile, we continued to lose altitude and by the time we reached the English Channel we were about 100 feet from getting wet. We threw everything overboard except 100 rounds for the top turret. The crew came forward and braced in the cockpit in case we ditched. There was no fuel left to transfer. We were lower than the lighthouse we flew by near the water. The throttle was set at 20 inches, 1,300 rpm. With just a little backpressure on the yoke and with a prayer, I eased the bird up and over the rim of the cliffs on the south shore of England. We landed on a runway at Chipping Nonga, which was still under construction. We begged for a few gallons of gasoline, which we got, and flew on to Molesworth after dark. Another bad mission was behind me. My nerves were showing the stress.

Mission # 18   9-19-43   Brussels, Belgium
No problems this time. My co-pilot was Lt. Paul Tibbets. Paul was lost on a later mission.

Mission # 19   9-23-43   Nantes, France
We bombed the submarine pens at Nantes France with only fair results. I saw eight fighters. The flak was moderate. It was a long haul, and we returned again after dark and nearly out of gas. A later run on these pens produced the desired results.

Mission # 20   9-27-43   Emden, Germany
Our target was Emden Germany. It was a very cold day. We were carrying single 1,000-pound bombs called "grapefruit" under each

wing. These bombs had wings which would fly them 20 miles to the target at 180mph. They would go through block buildings before exploding.

Certain aircraft were equipped with special radio receivers that could detect radio beacons placed at various sites. These signals enabled the "Pathfinder" aircraft to navigate above the clouds and to let us know when we were over the target. We had these aircraft with us on this run.

On the way there we lost the #3 engine but we made it to the target. Since there was complete cloud cover we dropped our bombs on cue from the Pathfinder aircraft. This mission lasted six hours and twenty minutes, mostly in the dark and cold.

Sometimes after missions the men would take off on passes to London, trying to forget the war. Getting a ride to Bedford or Kettering in the back of a GI truck, always taking their goodies along – ladies silk stockings for the Piccadilly Commandos to get their favors (some particularly brazen prostitutes who sold their services in London), or gum for the children who would come up to the uniformed Americans saying, "Gum, gum?" Cigarettes also bought wartime favors. Relaxing in London or Bedford was the same; "shacking up" with women, drinking too much, visiting the Key Clubs or going to the Windmill theater. The men would wait to the last moment to return to the base and to combat. They just tried to live life to its fullest because you never knew when the enemy bullet would tear into you or into your ship, causing it to explode in a flash – you'd be gone, not even the dog tags would survive. Five miles up in the sky, cold as hell, slobbering on oxygen, swearing, fearful, adrenaline pumping, almost exhausted – that was real combat.

"As might be expected in such horrific conditions, great numbers of fliers began to experience one or more symptoms of emotional stress: insomnia, irritability, sudden temper flashes, inability to concentrate, withdrawal from friends, nausea, weight loss, dizziness, blurring of vision, heart palpitations, Parkinson-like tremors, sexual impotence and aggressiveness, binge drinking, terrify-

ing battle dreams and horribly vivid nightmares. A later study found that virtually every flier who completed a tour of duty suffered from one or more symptoms of combat fatigue. Most of these men suppressed their anxieties and continued to fly.

The key person in the Air Force's medical chain of command was the flight surgeon, one of them serving each squadron on a bomber base. When a man broke in combat or showed dangerous signs of cracking, he was initially diagnosed and treated by his flight surgeon, who may or may not have had psychiatric training. These trained healers tried to get as close to the men as a chaplain would to his flock, making themselves available for counseling and medical treatment at all hours of the day and night. They were also military officers whose principal duty was to keep the men healthy and sane enough to fight for their country. It was a difficult road to walk.

The attempt was made to treat as many men as possible on base. If the flight surgeon detected mild emotional distress, he could send a war weary man for a week's rest at one of the English country estates that the Air Force had commandeered and turned into recovery centers for its fliers. The men dubbed these centers, "Flak Farms." (1)

And so it was that at this point, after Carl's 20th mission, the S. Q. flight surgeon determined that he and his crew needed a break. In October they were sent to a Flack Farm. The three-story mansion was staffed with Red Cross volunteers and had a butler and servants. There was good fresh food and hot running water for the men. While Carl was there he made friends with some local people who invited him to go on a foxhunt. He rode sidesaddle and had a good time. One woman kept referring to him as a "Colonial" to which Carl replied, "We're not Colonials any more. We whipped you folks back in 1776!"

During Carl's stay at the Flak Farm a second major run on Schweinfurt was held. Carl and another officer climbed a hill near the house to watch the bombers as they returned from Schweinfurt. It was a sad sight. The planes were scattered all over the sky. There was no real formation. The other officer called his base to check in. The news was not good.

The second bombing mission to the German city of Schweinfurt would be forever known as "Black Thursday" for the combat aircrews and supporting ground personnel of the 1st and 3rd Air Divisions; flying from sixteen airbases in England. Of the 291 bombers that were dispatched on October 14, 1943, twenty-six aircraft turned back to England due to mechanical or equipment problems. Thirty-six bombers were shot down on the way to Schweinfurt, and an additional 24 bombers were lost after leaving Schweinfurt.

Carl's days at the Flak Farm ended on a sour note.

Mission # 21   10-20-43   Duren Germany
Back to work. Our group's target was Duren Germany. Our bomber flew the #3 position. We had to drop our bombs on cue from the Pathfinder since the weather was bad all the way to 30,000 feet. Right after the drop we turned left and were attacked by 15 fighters. S/Sgt. Bill Addison, my top turret gunner, got an ME-109 just south of Rotterdam, Holland.

Mission #22   11-3-43   Wilhelmshaven Germany
The mighty Eighth Air Force had mustered over 1,000 bombers for this mission, the largest to date. I flew ship number 482, leading the B flight, second element. This armada stretched out for 20 miles. "Stacked" in high, low, and lead positions were the groups of the 1st, 2nd, and 3rd Divisions. Some have said that 25,000 men were involved in this mission, which seems plausible to me. It will never happen like that again! Houses below shook from the vibrations

caused by all these planes. It took a long time for all these units to pass by overhead. We were mighty surprised and relieved to see our P-38 fighter planes for our escort! They gave us grand cover for most of the trip.

Mission # 23   11-5-43   Gelsenkirchen Germany, Ruhr Valley
I flew in number 483 leading the second element in the top squadron. There was lots of flak. The ship on my right wing had been hit. The trailing edge of his left wing was on fire. Red flames ate along the wing toward the gas tanks. I waved for the pilot, Lt. Grant, to leave formation and bail out. He did not. He was determined to get to the target. They never made it.

Mission # 24   11-26-43   Bremen, Germany
It was a cold, wet, dreary day. Lt. Steve Gibson, our bombardier, was on his 25th mission, after which he would hopefully move on up to headquarters.

The lead ship in front of me took a direct hit in the nose section. The front of his aircraft came off, killing his navigator. His plane pressed down on top of me. I had to leave formation to avoid collision. Pieces of debris littered the sky. I was shook. Too many trips and now this! My nerves were so shot I dared not rejoin the formation. Then, one by one, our guns froze up and we were all alone. We were a straggler, and so vulnerable, that I knew I had to get back into formation. At last I managed to move up parallel with the group, and we flew back to England that way.

At long last, it was time for that 25th and final mission.

The events that happened on Carl Fyler's 25th and final mission were to change his life forever.

By the time November of 1943 had arrived I was really beginning to feel the effects of the stress of war. My nerves were almost shot. Just getting in the plane and making it fly was a huge effort, let alone flying in battle conditions. A person could only endure so much ...

The night after my 24th mission, the first to Bremen Germany, I was in a bad way. I was exhausted. I was completely wrung out. But I was hungry. So I drug myself up to the mess hall for supper.

I went through the line and got my food, so tired that it really didn't register with me what was slapped on my tray. It didn't really matter. I took the tray, set down, and began to eat. After a minute I looked up to notice that a handsome man was sitting across from me, wearing his officer greens, captains bars, and silver wings. It entered my mind that I was indeed eating supper with the famous movie star turned pilot, Clark Gable.

"Gable had enlisted shortly after the death of his wife, Carole Lombard. He wanted to be a machine gunner, he told a reporter, "where the going is really hot." Hap Arnold refused to give Gable a regular combat assignment, but when Gable heard that Arnold wanted him to be part of a project that filmed the air war for history and for recruitment purposes, he was not disappointed in the assignment. Gable knew that filming the air war would be nearly as dangerous as fighting it. "It's murder up there," he told one of his film crew, "They're falling like moths. They are dying like moths up there."

The other pilots didn't accept Gable's presence when he first showed up on the scene. They saw him as a pampered Hollywood hotshot, totally unsuitable for the battle missions he would face. Gable knew he had what it took, and he decided to prove them wrong. For starters, he accepted the same pay as the other pilots – $320 per month. He had made 100 times that when shooting the movie "Gone With The Wind." He surprised everyone by going out on the toughest runs. On one mission Gable was nearly killed when a shell tore through his plane and blew the heel off of his boot." (1)

By now, though, the man sitting across the table from Carl that night was no longer Clark Gable, Hollywood superstar. He was just another airman.

Under normal circumstances I would have struck up a conversation with Gable, but I just didn't have any conversation in me that night. The long silence didn't matter though. Gable knew from experience why I had no words for him. He too, had no conversation left. It was all we could do to get the forks to our mouths. We ate in silence until another man came and sat down with us. "Jesus Christ, the flak was heavy today," the man said. That was the extent of the dinner conversation that night.

I left the mess hall with some of my buddies and we headed out into the deep darkness, a darkness made worse by the blackout conditions. Suddenly, as we walked along in silence, a Jeep came barreling down the road, and not seeing us walking in the dark, the driver plowed right into us. I took a direct hit. My body flew up through the air like a rag doll across the Jeep. I landed on my left leg on the other side. The poor panicked driver turned on the headlights, jumped out and rushed around the jeep, calling out, "I am so sorry, I didn't see you, I am so sorry!" As the driver hustled me into the jeep, I saw my broken watch lying on the ground. The jeep had hit me so hard it had knocked the watch clean off of my wrist. The jeep driver rushed me to the infirmary, apologizing all the way.

The clock said 2 AM. It was November 29, 1943. I was asleep in my bed, still recuperating from being hit by a jeep three days before. I was in a fitful sleep when the officer of the day started shaking my shoulders, saying, "Get up Sir. You are flying today." No, I am not, " I growled back. "I am staying in bed and convalescing from being run down at night by the Squadron Jeep. Go away!" But the earnest young man keep insisting, so I got up and dressed and went to the headquarters in the dark. Sure enough, there was my name on the assignment list. I was scheduled to lead the high squadron. Some dark thoughts went through my mind. I ate some breakfast, gathered up my gear and headed out.

I learned in briefing that I had been assigned B-17G #42-29498-D, named "Dark Horse." It was combat mission number 84. Our target city was once again Bremen Germany, where we would be doing PFF (Pathfinder Force Bombing). It was scheduled to be a 6-hour mis-

sion. We would be carrying 8-50 lbs. G.P. (General Purpose) bombs and 20 xM47A1 incendiaries. We would be flying at a bombing alt. of 27,700 feet.

This would be my 25th and final credited mission. Somehow I knew that it was not going to be a good day.

As the Jeep pulled up toward the plane, Carl looked around at the scene before him. He had a sense of it all being very surreal. The ground crew was scurrying around the planes like an army of ants preparing the birds for their flight. The smell of the fuel permeated that air ... a smell that would stay in his memory forever. Time seemed to be going fast and slow all at once. Carl saw each of his crew as they stepped up to the plane that day, each one forever etched in his mind.

2nd Lt. Robert C. Ward
1st Lt. George Molnar
2nd Lt. J. S. Petrolino
T/Sgt. William J. Addison
Sgt. Ray B. O'Connell
S/Sgt. Raymond D. Ford
S/Sgt. Martin G. Stachowiak
S/Sgt George C. Fisher
S/Sgt. Joseph R. Sawicki

Steve Gibson had finished his 25th mission and been reassigned. Jack Jillson had been reassigned to HQ. Therefore James Petrolini would fly as his bombardier and Joseph Sawicki would be his tail gunner. In addition, a photographer Carl had never met named N.P.S. Egge had been assigned to fly with them that day.

Carl had taken a real liking to the soft-spoken Polish gunner Joseph Sawicki. Sawicki had flown with him on a couple of other missions, and Carl felt confident with him in the tail gunner position. Sawicki's parents had immigrated to the United States before Joseph was born. He had been born and raised in Detroit, and was proud to be an American and proud to be Polish. Sawicki did not like what he had seen going on in Europe and he was appalled at what happened when Hitler rolled in to his homeland. So when he was only 18 years old he had gone and enlisted in the Polish RAF. He was placed in the 300 Squadron. The fearless Sawicki was already been a hero during the war. After seven missions with the Poles he had earned the Polish Cross of Valor. This would be Joseph's 13th USAAF mission.

As the men stood around waiting for the flares, they were nervous. Carl's sense of foreboding grew with each passing minute, and as his concerns increased, so did the uneasiness of his crew. Finally the flares went green and the men climbed aboard the ship and the engines roared. As soon as his hands touched the throttle, Carl's mind set on the task before him. As always, he would focus on doing the job he was supposed to do, and bring his crew back safely.

"The outbound climb after departing the English coast was excessively fast, causing three of the B-17s to lose the formation and drop out. Dense and persistent contrails were encountered above 17,500 feet over the North Sea and Continent. There was a thick cloud cover over the Continent in three layers up to 25,000 feet. The lead Group was flying too low, forcing the 303rd to fly in the overcast. Many windshields, noses and guns iced due to the extremely cold temperatures. P-47 fighter support arrived as the bombers crossed the enemy coast. The lead Combat Wing fired a red flare, but failed to drop any bombs. At this time flak appeared and fighters were encountered after passing through the flak area. After several sharp turns, bombs were released on the Combat Wing leader's orders. They landed about twelve miles west of the city of Bremen. Fighter attacks from every direction became persistent. Many used the excessive contrails to sneak up on the formation. Rockets were fired into the formation from sev-

eral directions. JU-87s were spraying the formation with 20mm cannons, firing from the back seat flexible guns. Enemy aircraft closed in to 50 yards and gunners were unable to see them due to frost." (303rd)

It was hell in the sky on that cold November day.

As we approached our target over Bremen only two planes were left in the top squadron. That did not bode well. As we dropped our bombs on our target below, both planes were hit with flak. The Dark Horse abruptly lurched upwards.

The first burst of enemy fire hit co-pilot Bob Ward in the face causing his right eye to blow out. He slumped over the controls bleeding profusely. I pushed him out of the way as I had to have complete freedom to all of the ship's controls if I was to get the ship back. At last he stirred by himself, unbuckled his safety belt and left his seat. He sat on the floor, covering his wounded eye with his hand, blood gushing through his fingers. He was trying to stay out of the way, so that if I should need aid to fly the plane the engineer could leave his turret and help on the co-pilot's controls. At that instant, the ship was again hit by enemy fire. … S/Sgt. Bill Addison, the top turret gunner, was hit and wounded in the thigh. He was slammed out of his turret and came crashing down onto the flight deck landing across Ward as he sat there on the floor. It was awful to see the two wounded men tangled there on the floor, but I was so busy trying to fly the plane I couldn't help them. Another burst hit our tail section. The ship lurched up violently. I didn't know it then, but at that moment, both waist gunners had been tossed upwards then slammed to the floor. Our two engines on the right wing were damaged. Both shut down and I feathered the props. The right stabilizer and part of the right wing was gone as well. The third engine caught on fire. I was now flying a plane with only one engine on the left wing. The ship nosed up, turning to the right. I was fighting with every ounce of my being to keep the nose down.

Suddenly a German fighter came in, a head-on attack. His tracers streaked through the ship. Glass shattered, as his bullets tore through the cockpit. Pieces of steel went through my right shoulder and I felt sick, sick enough to faint. I felt the blood running down my arm to drip onto the floor below my seat. The aroma of death filled the cockpit as the fortress jerked, violently beginning to slowly turn on its side. Debris was flying ... there was the muffled sound of my crew yelling ... the sound of shrapnel flying all over, ripping away human flesh as non-stop 20mm rounds were fired at us ... It was like a twister from hell and an earthquake all at the same time.

All of a sudden I could hear my mother's voice, hear her parting words to me, "Carl, be so careful, I'm scared that you'll be killed, you know your Uncle Carl was killed in France in the last war, and to lose you in this war would kill me."

Determined not to give up, I sat up and tried again and again with the throttle to regulate the course of the damaged burning ship.

The thought of how bad things were in the back of the plane raced through my mind. I grabbed the interphone and tried to call my crew in the back of the plane, over and over. "Fisher! Marty! Sawicki! Anybody! Answer me! Report! Report!" It was no use. The inter phone had quit working. At that point I knew in the pit of my stomach that the ship was going to go down. I became single minded. I knew that I had to hold that plane in the air long enough for all that were able to get out to get out.

At last I saw that I could not control the ship at all. I turned to the two wounded men on the floor. Both were part way sitting up, and wide eyed they watched me, their eyes telling me that they had no hope that we could keep going. They were waiting for my next orders. I waved to abandon the ship. They helped each other to snap on the chest packs to their harness.

When I looked again both were gone. They must have bailed out through the escape hatch. Without realizing it, I whispered prayers for the men, mixed liberally with cuss words for the Germans. I prayed they would reach the ground safely, and receive the medical help they needed.

In the back of the plane, things were not going any better.

"Sawicki had been struck by a flak burst that tore away his left arm below the elbow and that also inflicted mortal wounds to his midsection. Bleeding profusely and in unimaginable pain, he crawled forward to the waist section to find both waist gunners, Fisher and Stachowiak, wounded and dazed on the floor of the aircraft. They had suffered multiple wounds and each had a broken arm.

With his last ounce of energy, Sawicki managed to buckle a chest pack chute on each and drag them to the waist door. Pulling the hinge-pin cable, he kicked out the door and wrestled both gunners to the exit, literally booting them out of the faltering aircraft into the minus 50 C air outside. They were able to pull their own ripcords and safely parachuted into enemy territory. Sawicki collapsed from his wounds and went down with the flaming Fortress. Sawicki's final actions in life were to go above and beyond the call of duty so that he could save the lives of his fellow crewmen." (303rd)

Still struggling to keep the massively damaged plane flying, I prayed to God that everyone who could get out had. I kept trying with all my might to steer the plane to the west as we turned on our side, but she refused to budge in that direction. I could hear the one .50 cal. gun still firing in the nose of the plane but it was firing very slowly. It did not sound like a machine gun. It sounded like it was playing the rhythms of a death march. The ship began a downward spiral to the right. I looked out the window. I could see the ground, and it was rotating. My insides lurched. It was time to get out.

I set the throttles and unbuckled my safety belt, grabbed my small chest pack, and snapped it on. I popped of the cords to my electric gloves, throat mike and head set. I slid down into the sticky pool of blood on the floor and crawled under the cockpit to see if the gunner there had gotten out. He was gone, and so was the door to the hatch, so I dropped myself out of the hatch as well. I clipped the tail section of the plane and then popped out about 15 feet behind her. The Dark

Horse continued downward to her death. I didn't know for sure, but the sickness in my gut told me that she took some of my crew with her. I reached for the rip chord on my chute, grappling in panic when I couldn't find it at first. At last I found the cord and pulled it. Nothing happened. I yanked again, harder, and the handkerchief-sized chute appeared, followed finally by the large main canopy. When that canopy opened it snapped so hard and so fast that my heels hit my shoulder blades. Then out of nowhere came a German fighter. He flew straight at me. I tried to swing myself in my 'chute, but I was so tired that I just hung there. The fighter came at me, then lifted his wing and passed me by. A second or so later I heard his guns as he poured a burst of machine gun fire into the doomed plane. Falling faster, I looked up at the canopy of my 'chute. It was parted, half of the canopy on each side. It had split in half when the fighter had made a pass at me. Looking down in horror, I saw the tops of the trees coming up at me.

I closed my eyes and breathed a three-word prayer: "God help me!" When I woke up I was lying in the middle of a path through the woods, parachute silk and tree branches all about me. I was bloody and injured, but I was alive ...

When my wits returned I looked above me to discover that I had taken all the branches off of one side of a 60-foot pine tree with my backside, doing more damage to the spot where the Jeep had hit me a few days before. I realized the tree had saved my life by breaking my fall. I cut the shroud cords and freed myself from the parachute. I tucked the cords into my pocket, knowing every little thing could potentially be of use to me in what I was about to face. I made my way to a nearby railroad bridge. I crawled under the bridge and destroyed the codes that I carried. I rested for a few minutes then I took off running, as best I could with my injuries. But it really didn't matter that I couldn't run fast. There really was no place to run. All of Europe was German territory in 1943...

It wasn't long before the Jerries captured me. One wore a spiked WWI helmet. He was missing an arm, but he carried a 10 gauge shot gun. There were three others with him. My back and one leg were *causing me quite a lot of pain. I was limping. I was taken to some flak barracks near the village of Delmenhorst. I met the FW-190 pilot who fired on me. His wingmen came in and photographed me. He told me he had 300 destroyed Allied aircraft to his credit. He said he had lived in the United States and had worked for the Pepsi-Cola Company. He wore a beautiful blue Luftwaffe officer's uniform complete with a chest full of medals.*

I was placed in a room with my wounded copilot Lt. Bob Ward. Using Pig Latin so the guards wouldn't understand me, I suggested to him that we break through a big window and escape into the timber. He said he did not feel up to it. I ate the candy in my escape kit so the Germans couldn't have it. I also hid the compass in my mouth. They got the silk maps and the money though.

I was taken from the flak barracks and put in a small pickup truck with a covered bed and driven through the night to a German camp where I was ordered into a darkened concrete room – an underground dungeon. Here were 10 big angry Air Force gunners. They were quite loud and upset over their capture. As the only officer present, I told them to calm down or things would get bad. They then sat on the floor and became quiet.

As my eyes became accustomed to the darkness I saw a body in the rear of the cell. I investigated and saw a blond sergeant of slight build in Air Force fatigues with a squashed head. His head looked like a watermelon that had been dropped. I inquired about him and was told he was a B-24 tail gunner who rode his ship's tail gun section to the ground from 24,000 feet after it broke apart from the bomber. I could not just let him lie there and die so in my best high school German I asked the guard at the door for things to patch up the wounded man's head. The guard brought me a small pan of water, some long strips of paper bandages, and some small scissors. I raised the man to a sitting position and began to clean the wounds. The paper bandages were not useful in binding the wounds, but I did my best to staunch the flow of blood. I never knew what happened to him after that because I was soon ordered out of the cell and off to a single cell with a very bright light bulb that burned continually. There was a wooden workbench that served as a bunk. There was fresh blood on the hard wooden slats. I was so tired. I lay down on the bloody bench and tried to sleep.

"Rat-a-tat-tat" Three machine gun bursts close by. I jumped up. I wondered what was going on so I climbed up on the bench and tried to look out, but the windows were too high. The shooting continued all night.

Next day I was marched to the railroad station in Bremen. I had to carry an American officer who had broken both ankles when he parachuted. We were taunted by a crowd of civilians; "Schweinhund! Terrifliger!" (Terror flyers) The mob cried out to the guards to "hang the Chicago gangsters!" My mind was working in a million ways, trying to see if there was any way to escape. Our CO had always told us that it was our sworn duty to escape if possible. However, no wise options were available.

Soon the guard and I boarded the train. We were in a civilian rail car with other passengers. We rode for quite a while. He gave me black bread and sausage. I ate the sausage. I left the sawdust black bread on the train as it burned in my stomach. At one stop I was given a warm cup of pale weak yellow tea.

We arrived at Dulag Luft interrogation center at Oberursel, a few miles north of Frankfurt. I was put in a small white cell with no door handles and no windows. I spent three difficult weeks in solitary confinement. All around me I could hear constant screaming and hollering and singing in the other cells. Some men were driven insane. It was here that I learned a skill that would prove to be useful again and again in life. I learned to mark time. All I had to do was survive for one minute, then I could go on to the next. If I could survive for one minute at a time, I could wait for one hour, wait for one day to pass. This helped me to stay sane in an insane situation. I exercised the best I could to keep my injured body as limber as possible. Every so often, a small door on the floor opened, and through it would appear a pan of stew made with unidentifiable ingredients and a spoon. When I was finished I would push it back out, and it would be passed on the to the other prisoners of war.

After 3 weeks of this preparation, I was taken to the interrogation room, where I was questioned for 7 hours. I was interrogated by a German doctor named Haas, whom I suspect was a psychiatrist. I told him that I was an "oberst" when they asked me my rank. I did not know at the time that that meant "colonel," but I figured that I would make their intelligence department work and that perhaps I might get better treatment. However, the German already knew all about me – about my family, my missions, my friends who had been shot down, even how they died! The doctor laughed at me and said he knew exactly what rank I was, and that I had been promoted to captain. He threw the captain's bars at me! Later I would find out that he was correct, that I had been promoted. It seems the Germans knew more about me than I did!

Sometime later I was moved to a barbed wire prison at the IG Farbin Industry building in the city park in Frankfurt. IG Farbin was a synthetic dye and chemical company that cooperated closely with Nazi officials throughout the war and later produced synthetic oil and rubber at Auschwitz. This company also held the patent for the pesticide Zyklon B, which was used in the gas chambers at concentration camps. The Germans were quite anxious to protect this factory, and what better way to do that than to put Allied POW officers there to prevent the factory from being bombed? It was here that I finally received a decent meal and a shower. It was also here that I discovered that I had two more wounds in my upper left thigh. I dug the steel shrapnel out of those wounds as well as other fragments in my left arm and on both hands. I never did see a German medic for any of my injuries.

My uniform was literally in shreds after my parachute jump so it seemed quite urgent to repair it. A fellow POW loaned me a needle. I unraveled some cloth in my room and used the thread to sew up my uniform.

After my stay in Frankfurt, 42 of us were loaded into two boxcars by guards armed with machine guns and dogs. We were chained in a *boxcar, a cold 140 x 8 feet of space. When we left the station we became like a real traveling circus – a real sideshow, a big attraction at all the bombed out cities. We rode for 5 days to Berlin, sitting on the cold floor in brutal winter weather.*

Sometimes they would stop the cars and open the doors and let us relieve ourselves. No other provisions were made for us. We saw lots of damage from our bombing. I saw bathtubs hanging by their pipes from the 5th or 6th floors of buildings. Berlin was badly damaged by that time. We had a 3-day showing in Berlin, the week of Christmas. The train pulled up at the station and they would open the door to the boxcar so people could look at us. Children and old folks alike came out to stare at us, shake their fists at us and spit on us and call us Chicago gangsters.

Some of the RAF officers in the boxcar who were Jewish asked me to throw their dog tags out of the boxcar. I hesitated to do it because a soldier without his identification was considered a saboteur by the Germans and was shot on the spot. But I did as they asked when the boxcar doors were opened next. Perhaps it would be better to be found without dog tags by the Germans than to be found Jewish.

In three weeks time, we arrived at our destination – Stalag Luft 1. I was now officially a prisoner of war.

There was a letter in the mailbox! It was from Carl! Ellen Jean had not heard from Carl for several weeks, and she was beginning to get worried, but this letter would allay her fears. However, when she pulled the pale blue paper out of the envelope, she knew the writing was not Carl's. It was actually from Carl's good friend and crewmate, Steve Gibson. Why would he be writing to her? A silent alarm bell began clanging in the back of her mind. She felt the emotion drain out of her as she read the letter. She felt hollow on the inside, like someone had taken a sharp knife and gutted her. Woodenly, she went to find her mother in law. She found Helen in the kitchen starting supper. Ellen Jean stuck the letter in her hand. The look that crossed her mother-in-law's face made Ellen Jean feel even more sick to her stomach. The news was not good.

December 5, 1943

Dear Ellen Jean,

You have surely been notified by now by the government that Carl and crew are missing. I have hopes of hearing from them soon and will cable you as soon as I hear from or about them.

I personally packed their clothes and turned them over to the government and they in time will mail them to you. His personal belongings will be mailed to you at once by me.

Sincerely,
Steve Gibson

The official telegram informing them that Carl was missing in action came a few days later. Within a few months, they got word from the Red Cross that Carl was a prisoner of war. The family's worst fears had been realized.

1944

As the New Year rolled in Carl Fyler was in a place he had always hoped to avoid. As he lay on his hard wooden bunk in barrack number 3 North Unit of Stalag Luft 1, his desolation and his longing for home was nearly too much to bear. He thought of his mother, his father, his sister his wife … of his home in Kansas, the golden wheat fields and the ranches with their rolling hills and grazing cattle … so far away from this hellhole. He sighed and turned over, trying to find a comfortable spot that would not make his injured leg ache. He had learned to mark time in the Dulag. He would mark time again. And in the meantime, if he could figure out how to escape, by God he would.

Real sleep was a thing of the past too. Even if he could get comfortable on this miserable bed, his mind wouldn't let him sleep. Over and over, he replayed in his mind the downfall of Dark Horse. The sensations of the plane in its death throes, the screams and cursing of his men, the sound of the guns firing, the bullets and shrapnel ringing through the plane, the metallic smell of blood and the stench of death

… it was, and would be forever, a scene emblazoned in his mind. There was sharp anxiety about his crew. He could account for only three of his crew: He knew that Lt. James Petrolino, his new bombardier, Lt. Bill Ward, and Lt. George Molnar had all been taken POW. Beyond that he knew nothing. He would run their names over and over in his head: Addison, O'Connell, Ford, Stachowiak, Fischer, Sawicki, and the photographer, Egge. Where were they? Had they lived or died? It was agonizing to him that he could not get any information about them. He lay awake, wondering.

He remembered his march to Stalag Luft 1. The train stopped in the city of Barth, Germany and they were unchained and unloaded from the boxcar as if they were so many head of cattle. There were guards armed with machine guns and guard dogs lining both sides of the tracks. They were paraded through the town, through the arched tower at the gates, past the large Lutheran church that he could see from his barracks on a clear day, and past the building he would later learn was the flak school … where women learned how to fire the antiaircraft guns that would take down the Allied flyers. He remembered as they approached the gates the sick fear he felt in his stomach. He knew he was marching through the gates of hell on earth.

Stalag Luft 1 was located just outside of Barth Germany on a narrow finger of land that jutted out into the Baltic Sea. A large pine forest bordered the camp on the western side and to the east and to the north the icy waters of the sea lapped at the land, less than a mile from the barbed wire fence that marked the edge of the world for the prisoners housed in the camp. At its peak, the number of prisoners held there would reach 8,500.

That barbed wire snaked around the camp for miles, in two rows four feet apart, attached to 10-foot posts. In the two-foot space between fences were lose wire coils. The barbs on the wire were very long, very sharp, and in clusters of four. There was a single strand of barbed wire that ran around the fence about shoulder height. This wire was the warning wire. If any man touched this wire he was in danger of being shot at once. Every hundred yards there was a guard tower armed with a machine gun and a pair of spotlights that could turn the night into day. There was nowhere a person could go and not be in the sights of the men in those towers.

The camp was divided into compounds. There were four such prisoner compounds. The fifth area was for the German staff. Called the Oa-

sis by the prisoners, the area consisted of neat buildings surrounded by green grass. This was in sharp contrast to the prisoner compounds, which sported bare earth and shabby barracks.

Since the men in Stalag Luft 1 were pilots and officers, they received much better treatment than did the enlisted men, as dictated by the Geneva Convention standards established after WWI. Even so, internment brought suffering beyond belief; the unending frigid weather, the unpredictable behavior of the guards. Inadequate food, lice, sickness, boredom, death by starvation or by exposure, was the everyday life of the imprisoned men. The German word for prisoner of war is Kriegesgefangenen.

They called themselves "Kriegies."

Soon Carl and his barrack mates fell into a depressing routine. The Kriegies were counted twice a day. Each barracks would line up in a formation of four rows, with the senior officer, or "barracks commander" standing in front just as the commander of an infantry company would do. Carl was the senior officer in his barrack, due to the fact that he had been First Lt. longer than anyone else in his group. (Carl was actually a captain at this point, though he did not know that for sure.) All the barracks of each compound were grouped around an open area so that they could all be counted in series without the guards losing sight of any of them. While the outside prisoners were being counted, one prisoner would remain in each barracks, along with any prisoners who were too sick to stand outside. A guard would walk through each barracks and count the number of men in them, accompanied by that one prisoner whose job it was to see that the guard didn't steal anything.

After the role call, the men had the day to themselves. Since they were officers, the Geneva Convention stated they could not be used for slave labor, so the men were left to entertain themselves. Boredom and too much time to think took a toll on many of the men. They could do art or read whatever books they could find. There were worship services, ball games and boxing matches. There was even a camp newspaper and a band and a theater group!

The Germans would let the men shower only occasionally. Twenty men would line up at the gate to head over to the shower building. Carl relished the chance to clean his battered body, but always harbored the secret fear that one day the showerheads would not emit water, but the lethal gas that the folks in the concentration camps got. Luckily they always got water, but not much. Each man was allowed one minute of water to soap up, if a person had soap, then another minute to rinse off. Then they would dry, dress, and return to camp. Sometimes not all 20 men in his group would come to the shower, so Carl would get back in line and go for a second shower on those days. Four minutes of water was a real luxury at Stalag Luft 1.

Other bathroom facilities were primitive. A large barrel was used for a latrine in the barracks. Outside there were straddle latrines that leeched into the underground water supply. There was never any toilet paper provided; the men had to improvise. Russian slave labor was used to haul out the waste from latrines, in tanks on horse-drawn carriages they called "honey wagons." The Russians would ladle the excrement up with a long handled dipper that reached into the tanks. Dipperful by dipperful, they would empty the latrines.

There was a Concentration Camp for Russians next to ours. The people in that camp had it hard. The Germans were brutal to them. I saw young Russians working in the cold and snow to repair bombed-out railroads. Sometimes they would come up to our fence and stare in at us as if they wished they were with us. Their fingers were swollen, their faces without feeling; a deadpan stare. I felt sorry for them, and yet I too was a prisoner of war, also facing the unknown. The women were brought down to shower in the building next to our camp. They were marched naked in the snow. They showered like we did – one minute of water, wait, then one more minute of water. Then they were marched back.

The windows of the barracks were shuttered every day at 4:00 in the afternoon and left that way until the next day. The men were to stay in the barracks unless they had a very good reason to go elsewhere. There was a single 10-watt light bulb in the room. The men were allowed to have the light on from 4 p.m. until 8p.m. Sometimes the German guards would crawl under the barracks to listen to Kriegie conversations for their Intelligence service. When the men knew they were listening, some very tall stories would be told! Also, the latrine buckets were sometimes spilled ...

The men were on their own to find clothing. Carl's tattered uniform quickly became unusable. He was able to find a blue RAF uniform, which fit well, except he had to lap the belt around once to hold the pants up, he had lost so much weight. If he had been found dead along the road in this uniform, as so many service men were after the war, they would have thought he was British and sent him to England for identification. He also had no coat, his bomber jacket having been destroyed in his fall. Later he bought one from a Texan for 200 cigarettes. Cigarettes were the exchange medium in the camp.

Medical care was minimal, and provided by other prisoners with few other proviions for care. A Dr. Nichols, who had been captured at Dunkirk, removed Bob Ward's eye, which had been damaged beyond salvaging when the shell blew up in front of his face. Another time a man in Carl's barrack became gravely ill and in great pain. After three days Carl went to the gate and told the postern that a medical doctor was needed immediately. The man who came was a British Army dentist. Somehow, the dentist removed the ill man's appendix, and the man survived!

Getting enough to eat was a constant problem. The men existed on a diet that consisted mainly of rutabagas, grass soup and boiled barley, which could easily have been mistaken for wall paper paste. Each man received only one tin cup full. There was never any meat. The Red Cross would also send in food packages. The Kriegies did their own cooking. At times they would be issued just one and a half bricks of pressed coal dust to cook for 28 men. Other times there was nothing.

In order to cook as efficiently as possible, we improvised something we called a Kriegie Stove. The stove had a burner made out of tin cans and a blower that was driven by a hand crank made of tin can lids. The crank was connected to the blower with shoelaces. This arrangement would heat a bucket of water or coffee with just a handful of wood or coal chips or whatever else we could scrounge. We would dream about food and the meals we would eat when the war was over. Often we would watch the large ravens that flew into the camp. They were about the size of a small frying chicken or game hen. We even thought about catching one of them to make "chicken stew," though I don't think anyone ever really caught one.

The Red Cross sent in tins of food, which were rationed out to the men. However the Germans were brutal in regards to this food. They intentionally punctured the Red Cross tins of food to ensure that it spoiled quickly. They thought we would horde the food for an escape. We ate whatever would spoil the quickest, and held off on the corned beef until last. There were green areas on the corned beef where the cans had been punctured, but we ate it anyway. The Germans counted the number of tin cans entering camp and the number going out.

The arrival of new prisoners in camp was always a red-letter day because it meant fresh news from the outside. Although the men had secretly improvised a radio that they listened to when they could, they were hungry for news from the outside, for news of the success of the war efforts and for news of family and crewmates. It was common that the Kriegies would line up around the fences near the main gates when new prisoners were being brought in, desperately searching for familiar faces and calling out for news. One dark, cold rainy day found Carl standing near the fence as a new group of prisoners were being led in. With a start, he recognized his flight engineer and top turret gunner, S/Sgt. Bill Addison. Bill was limping sideways through the main gate, obviously not in good shape. Carl ran to the fence and called out to him. Bill moved over next to the fence and they tried to talk as best they could. It was Carl's first opportunity to find out about the rest of his crew, and the news was not good.

When we were being shot down, a piece of .20mm shell passed through Bill's thigh and he was slammed out of his position onto the flight deck. I had ordered Bill to bail out, hoping that on the ground he would receive the medical attention that might save his life. When Bill was told to bail out, he elected to delay pulling his ripcord, falling several thousand feet before opening his canopy. He knew that the Germans often machine gunned airmen hanging in their chutes. What he hadn't counted on was that the force of his 'chute opening would nearly rip his wounded leg completely from his body. He landed and was promptly captured, along with our two waist gunners, Fisher and Stachowiak.

The medical attention I had hoped my men would receive had not been provided. The three of them were shipped via boxcar to Stalag Luft 4, which was in the Pomerania area of Poland. Food was so scarce there that the men lost 40 pounds or more. Some men lost as much as a pound a day. When the Russians began to advance on Poland, the Germans decided to move the POWs and captives in order to delay their liberation. This march was called "The Black March." The prisoners faced a 500-mile trek in blizzard conditions across

Germany, during which hundreds died. Due to Bill's bad leg he was unable to keep pace with the mass of marching men. He tried to continue in the rain and the snow by walking sideways. Even so he was a straggler. Finally the Germans took him off of the march. He was one of the lucky ones.

I now learned the complete story of the heroism shown by Joseph Sawicki in getting the two waist gunners, Fisher and Stachowiak, out of the plane at the cost of his own life. Bill knew that Fisher and Stachowiak were both still alive but in bad shape. Fisher had been reported repatriated back to the United States on a Red Cross ship. Addison told me that some of the men pried open the ball turret before they bailed out to discover that our turret gunner, Ray Ford, was dead from a string of machine gun fire. Stachowiak had been on the Black March for 86 days. During this time the guards bayoneted Stachowiak in his good arm and since he could not run they set the dogs on him during the march. Marty Stachowiak was 38 years old and had been starved down to 50 lbs. Bill had heard that four men were killed on the ground by some German civilians. I surmised that this included our radioman, Raymond O'Connell, and the photographer, Nellins Egge.

Bill looked so bad. All I could think of to do was to throw my RAF turtleneck sweater to him over the three fences. The Germans kept him in North Compound IV, where he had to sleep on the floor.

Carl now knew the basics of the fate of his crew. That knowledge brought him some minor degree of peace. At least he knew ...

<u>Killed in Action</u>
Joseph Sawicki
Ray Ford

<u>Bailed Out/POW</u>
Bob Ward
George Molnar
Bill Addison
James Petrolino

George Fisher (repatriated)
Martin Stachowiak

Bailed Out/Killed on Ground?
Ray O'Connell
Nellins Egge

It became Carl Fyler's mission to figure out how to escape from Stalag Luft 1. Carl had a quick, active mind that would chew on something until he figured it out. In his everyday life he would study a problem from all angles, taking all factors into consideration and evaluating the consequences before he acted on something. He put these traits to work in the camp. He often walked around the camp, getting exercise and watching closely every detail that went on, learning the routines of all the guards and commandants. He had even scoped out the locks on the shower room exit doors at one point, but determined escaping there was not good strategy. He also became very adept at scavenging and hording any small thing that might prove useful. Carl would often lay awake at night and work out escape routes in his mind. He was always on the alert for a chance to escape safely.

While we were at this camp we dug 87 tunnels, using tin cans as shovels. This would result in a lot of sand dug from the holes that we needed to dispose of! We would carry the sand from the tunnel in sacks inside the legs of our trousers, and dump it out on the grass during our perimeter walks. The level of the ground rose about 2 inches by the time we had dug 87 tunnels! We used the slats from our beds as reinforcements for the walls of the tunnels. The Germans used sound detectors to locate our tunnels. The Germans sent out men we called "ferrets" to find our tunnels and destroy them. They would also post two guards with a guard dog at the entrances of the ones they found. One time we caved our own tunnel in on top of a ferret, but they saved him. After the Germans found all 87 tunnels they erected a black grave cross with the number 87 on it over the last tunnel.

We also made plans to shoot the guard in the southeast tower and make a mass escape. The northeast tower guard was to be taken out by a captain fighter pilot who was also an Olympic archer. He made a homemade bow and arrow. We unraveled our webbed belts for the string for the bow. Wax was melted off of waxed paper to wax the bowstring. This plan never came to pass, however.

We gave our guards nicknames like "Butcher Boy," "Turkey Neck," "Big Stoop" and "Little Tish." Some of the guards were from the Luftwaffe and some were Wehrmacht soldiers. The Wehrmacht guards were quite old, perhaps WWI veterans. Some of the guards liked to trade with the soldiers. One night a German soldier did something even more amazing. He opened the shutter and passed me a pistol in its holster and a box of shells. "Was ist los, what's going on," I asked? I immediately passed the pistol and the box to the man standing behind me and told him to run and hide them, so he did!

One bright day I set some of the fence posts on the north side of camp on fire so I could pull off some of the barbed wire. We had used all the slats in our bunks to reinforce the tunnels we had dug, and so the beds were falling apart. I wanted to use the wire to support the beds. As the wire was pulled into the barracks we pulled it over the door lock catch to break the barbs off of the wire. "Butcher Boy" caught me in the act and put his big pistol up to my nose. I just sat down on the ground and hoped the fat sergeant wouldn't shoot! He held that pistol to my nose for what seemed like forever, then slowly put his gun back in his holster and walked away. I don't know why he didn't pull the trigger.

We also made a radio. A POW who had been taken to headquarters for punishment managed to steal a vacuum tube from the German commander's record player. We managed to get a drop of solder from a milk can we found in a Red Cross food parcel. We used these things to build a radio, and soon we picked up the news: "Dit dit dit dah, Dit dit dit dah, this is the BBC News, London." We would pass the news we heard from barracks to barracks with a runner.

In July of 1944 there was an assassination attempt on the life of Adolph Hitler. When the news came across on the BBC, we prema-

turely assumed the war was over. "Germany is kaput!" we cried and ran outside. The guards drew their machine guns down on us and said, "You have a radio!" They then proceeded to tear everything apart in the room, the bunks and even the floorboards. I held my pocketknife in my closed hand while they searched me, with my pants down around my ankles. I made it! I kept the knife!

Once after that they ran us out in the dark wet snow, into a barbed wire corral and left us there for three days. For three days I wiggled my toes in wet snow to keep them from freezing. There was no place to sit. It was terrible.

At one point Hitler wanted to renounce the international conventions relating to prisoners of war, and he wanted to execute all prisoners of war. The BBC quoted Dr. Bruckhardt, president of the International Red Cross when reporting the story. The doctor said that the Wehrmacht had refused to carry out the order.

Christmas Eve, 1944 was upon them, and all the men felt the aching melancholy of being in that place rather than at home with their loved ones. The men hoped that perhaps the camp personnel would give them some sort of special meal or treat on this holiday, but nothing changed. Same routine, same tasteless gruel – a day just like any other day. As it grew dark and the barracks grew cold, the depressed men went into their quarters and waited for the darkness to come.

Suddenly, someone called out, "The curfew is lifted for tonight! There is a Christmas Eve service in the next compound. Come on out!" The Kriegies couldn't believe their ears, but didn't hesitate in grabbing their coats – those who had one – and headed out the door. It was a clear cold night, and the snow crunched under their feet. Carl looked up into the night sky that he hadn't seen for nearly a year, and drew his breath in. He was stunned at the beauty he saw overhead. The stars hung in the crisp air like diamonds, and one large star, probably a planet, shone just overhead. As they walked, someone began to sing:

Silent Night, Holy Night, all is calm, all is bright …

It didn't take long before the whole company of men was singing that beloved Christmas carol. The German guards heard the sound, and stopped what they were doing. They knew that song. That song was their song too. They joined in the singing, in German, and soon the song lifted up into the sky, German and English blended together like two ribbons of sound and harmony intertwined.

Tonight they would sleep in peace. War and internment did not have the power to destroy the holiness of that special day.

Carl lay on the wooden bunk later that night, cold and sleepless again. His heart was sore as he thought of the wonderful Christmases he had had in Kansas with his family. He wondered when he would see them again. He thought about Ellen Jean, as he did every night. He spent some time, as he often did when sleep would not come, thinking about the house with the picket fence they would build when he got home. He wondered what they were doing at home in Hutchinson without him. And finally, he drifted off into a homesick sleep. A peace of sorts.

Life back in Kansas was not easy either. Despite the appearance that Helen Fyler and Ellen Jean may have put on while Carl was around, the two really did not get along well at all. Carl Fyler was the apple of Helen's eye, and she would do anything for him. Carl had told her to "keep an eye" on Ellen Jean, so keep an eye on her she would. As time passed, the physical proximity of the two women did not help. Helen was manipulative and controlling, and Ellen Jean was immature and bored. It did not make for all quiet on the home front.

By as early as January 1944, as Carl was becoming accustomed to his new life at Stalag Luft 1, Ellen Jean was growing restless living under the watchful eyes of the old woman she thought of as the "jailer." Life had gone from being a party with all the flyboys to being a drudge. Ellen Jean was lonely and she missed having a man around. Nowadays all she did was go to work and come home. If she went out with friends, which she did as often as she could to relieve the boredom, Mother Fyler would scowl at her, or worse, suggest to her or others around town that she was doing things that were improper for a married woman. When Ellen Jean complained to Carl of this in letters sent to Molesworth, he simply told her to "soldier it out." Ellen Jean wrote of her growing resentment and restlessness to her own mother. Her mother responded by saying,

Yes, I can imagine how Helen thinks you should act, but most of it is put on for she did all she could to make Carl unhappy when he got married just because she wanted him all to herself. I should think her conscience would hurt her now for at least she could have saved him some suffering. I am thankful I didn't fuss with him about it anyway. If you are going to be a comfort to him though I guess you really should sit down and cry for them. Carl knows how it is with you. He knows that you aren't having a swell time of it even though you do go out with the girls once in a while. I think you must be getting pretty restless …. Really Ellen Jean, I think if ever there was a time when you should stay put it is now. You may hear from Carl and you may not. Whether you do or not you have no way of knowing what minute he may be sent home. If he was disabled or too shaken up to do any more flying in the war you would want to be the one to be with him and help him get back to his old self again. I somehow think he wants you to stay here and wait for him too. I know you must be feeling terribly unsettled and at loose ends now for things are uncertain and up to now you have had Carl to help you plan things. You just have to carry on alone for the time being. I think after the war you might want to go to the farm for a month or so where you can think things out more clearly …

Ellen Jean burst into frustrated tears as she read her mother's words. If one more person told her to soldier up for Carl's sake she thought she would go mad. What about her? She was going mad in this stifling place anyway. And even though she knew it wasn't very Christian of her, she was beginning to hate her mother-in-law.

1944 wore on and on. There were infrequent Red Cross letters from Stalag Luft 1, but they weren't written by Carl, it wasn't his writing and it didn't even sound like what he would say. Ellen Jean later learned that there were German women in the camp who functioned as censors who would take the men's letters to change content and re-write them as they saw fit. It seemed as if this would go on forever. Who knew when or if Carl would ever be home? Who knew what kind of shape he might be in when he did get home? All Ellen Jean knew was that she couldn't stand living in this awful little town one minute longer. Ellen Jean was more unhappy than she ever had been in her life.

The one bright spot of the year happened in May, when Ellen Jean was asked to accept the war medals that Carl had earned. The newspaper article in the Great Bend KS newspaper on Monday May 15, 1944 read:

"Air Medal Presentation Made to wife of Fyler, Now German Prisoner"

Mrs. Ellen Jean Fyler, wife of Lt. Carl J. Fyler received the Air Medal and three oak leaf clusters for her husband at the Great Bend Army Air Field Saturday afternoon. The decoration was presented by Colonel Potter B. Paige, Commanding Officer of the Great Bend Base

presented the decoration. Mrs. Flyer came to Great Bend for the decoration from her home in Hutchinson. The three oak leaf clusters represent the second, third and fourth awards of the same decoration.

The presentation was made on the ramp and was witnessed by several formations of troops. Following the reading of the citation and the presentation of the decoration, the troops paraded in review in honor of Mrs. Fyler.

Lt. Fyler, now a prisoner of war in Germany, was a pilot of a Flying Fortress based in England. His aircraft was reported missing on its twenty-fifth mission over enemy territory on November 29, 1943. The twenty-two year old flyer had been in England since the first of June 1943.

His plane was apparently in serious trouble before it went missing according to information available. His waist gunner wrote to Mrs. Fyler, giving no details except to say, "If it weren't for him I wouldn't have been able to write this letter. I only wish I could do my last bomb run with him. Then I wouldn't have the slightest doubt that we would get back."

The citation, by direction from the President of the United States, reads as follows:

"For exceptionally meritorious achievement while participating in 20 separate bomber combat missions over enemy occupied continental Europe. The courage, coolness and skill displayed by this officer upon these occasions reflect great credit upon himself and the armed forces of the United States."

Accompanying the article was a fine photograph of the well-dressed Ellen Jean, posing for the camera as an officer pinned Carl's medals to her chest. On that day at least, Ellen Jean was proud to be Carl's wife.

However, within the week, Ellen Jean was upset with Helen Fyler again. On May 21, 1944, she wrote a note to her mother-in-law:

I am sorry if having my sister here to visit me inconvenienced you the way it did. I want you to know that what Margaret said wasn't meant to be against you personally. It was just her own opinion that I was doing good to live with people so different from myself. Margaret couldn't remember saying this to anyone but me in a letter. We looked at both sides of the matter and decided that it must be as hard for you to get used to me as it was for me to get used to you. If you would rather I live someplace else I can try to find some place to live while I go to business school this summer. I have tried to make you like me for myself and not treat me nice just because of Carl. I guess I have failed somewhere and I am really sorry because I have learned to like and worry about you the way Carl does. It is too bad that this whole misunderstanding can't be cleared up but I guess it never will be. Carl is the only person that might be able to do it but I doubt if he will as he doesn't like to think about it ...

Ellen Jean began to leave the house more and more to go to parties with friends. She didn't care any more what people thought. She just couldn't take one more moment locked up in that house with her husband's parents as her only companions. She needed more out of life ... she needed more laughter, and more excitement. What happened was probably inevitable. One night Ellen Jean met a man at one of the parties, a man with a quick laugh and flashing green eyes, a sailor from the Hutchinson Naval Air Training Base whose ginger colored hair earned him the nickname Red. Red was married. Ellen Jean would later write a letter to Red's wife:

In November Jim and Red came to live here. I met him at one of the Dillon's parties. From there I got to know Red better. We used to sit at the piano and sing songs and then we would talk. The situation with the Fylers and myself was beginning to drive me crazy. I felt as if my whole nervous system would crack any minute. I had kept my feelings to myself all this time, thinking perhaps when Carl got home it would all be all right. But now Red was there to listen. One night I started telling him all about it, and suddenly I was crying. I told him about everything that happened since Carl left me to go overseas. I cried and I cried. I cried so much I thought maybe I would never cry again.

From that time on I got so dependent on Red's humor, his understanding, his wonderful personality. He is as grand of a person as I have ever known. I respect him greatly, and he has never taken advantage of me.

It is very hard to convince people that our feelings for each other are only mental, that it is the feeling of companionship of two people trying to cheer each other the best that we know how.

Whether Ellen Jean and Red were having an affair or not is ultimately between the two of them, but the stage for disaster had been set. Carl didn't know it but he had more troubles than just the Germans.

1945
By 1945 conditions at Stalag Luft 1 had markedly deteriorated. As the wheels came off the German war machine they ceased making any attempt to provide for those in internment or concentration camps. Food and water supplies disappeared.

The spring of 1945 was difficult. The food ran out. The Germans quit pumping water to us. Hauptman Von Beck was the only decent German I met while in captivity. He said he was a professional soldier, just back from the Russian front. He was 80 years old and most emphatically stated that he was NOT a Nazi. He gave us a shovel and some concrete culverts and told us to dig a

well. We dug a well right in the parade ground. Over 8,000 men had used the straddle trenches for latrines, so the water needed to be sterilized. There was no way to make a fire to boil it. The only thing we could think of to do was to throw ashes into the well, and drink. There was not much water in the well anyway. We had to ration what there was. It was only about a cup per day per man.

The British and American troops were moving in from the west and the Russians were moving in from the east. It soon became apparent that the Russians would reach Stalag Luft 1 first. The German soldiers were terrified to be captured by the Russians. They knew what the retribution would be like. So when the Russian army began to close in on Stalag Luft 1 the guards abandoned the camp.

The Germans were right to be terrified of the oncoming Russians. They lived up to their reputation for brutality. The German civilians at Barth felt the wrath of the Russian Army. Their women and children were raped and killed on the porches of their own homes, and the men shot and tortured. Even though the war would soon be over the atrocities continued.

It was the morning of April 29, Easter Sunday, and a day I will never forget. The Russian advance parties arrived, slaughtering all the retreating bewildered Germans. There was gunfire all day. At last I came out of my foxhole in the prison compound with my hands above my head. In my best Russian I shouted at the Russian troops, "Americaski Lochich – American pilot!

As soon as the Russians caught on they smiled and crowded around us. We all shook hands. A bottle of something I was later to learn was vodka was passed around. I took a healthy swig. Molten fire ran down my throat and tears came to my eyes. The Russians laughed and tilted the bottle again in a toast to Roosevelt. Not to be outdone we returned their gesture by toasting Marshal Stalin. This we kept up until I knew I was about to pass out, drinking toasts to "our" Roosevelt and their Stalin. Having got out of the habit of drinking in the year and a half that I had been in Germany, my ability to hold liquor was greatly hampered. But, to keep face and not create a situation,

I kept on drinking, often making trips around the corner to heave up my toenails.

That night, around 2:00 AM I crept away from the celebration, sick and tired and vowing never to touch vodka or any other liquor ever again.

The German guards were gone. The Russians didn't seem to care if we stayed or left, but they weren't going to give us any food. We pushed the fences over down in the southeast corner by the guard tower and out we went! We never did use the gates.

We went scrounging for food. We found some Holstein cows. We herded them into a camp out north in the timber and butchered them for meat. I decided to go to the flak school building to look for food. No luck. Then I went to the air base. There were crashed German planes all over the field. I found a FW-190 fighter intact and parked in a concrete hanger. I crawled into the cockpit and read the German markings. I could not start the bird. So I ransacked the area for food. I finally found some rye crackers. These did not do much to abate the deep gut hunger. I gave some of them to the broomstick thin men in the French officers prison camp I found near the base. These men had been held by the Germans for 5 years. They were not really men anymore. They were just bones that had not quite finished dying. It was hard to see what was in that camp. There were dead bodies piled everywhere and the smell was horrible.

There were so many men and so little food. Food became our quest. One morning another man and I found a small boat and so we rowed it across the inlet of the sea over to the other side to see if any food could be found over there. We had no luck, so we started back. Suddenly shots rang out! Someone on the shore was shooting at us. I didn't know if it were German military, German civilians, or Russians. The war wasn't over yet!

On May 11 or 12, a British officer and I went back to the air base. This time we found a radio intact in a hangar. We strung a wire up to the top of the hangar for an antenna. We rummaged around some more and found some batteries, enough to make a transmission. The British officer used the radio transmitter key to make a call for help.

On May 13, a B-17 came flying in over the trees. I never heard a more beautiful sound. It landed on the cleared runway, taxied up to the hangar, and spun around. The pilot opened up the door and yelled out, "Thirty-five of you get on board," and so we did, in one mad scramble. This is how I finally got out of German territory. My navigator, Lt. George Molnar got out the same way the next day.

I stood between the pilot and the co-pilot as we skimmed the pines trees and headed out across Germany. I was free at last.

As the plane climbed over Aachen Germany, Carl could see the devastation from battle damage below him. It looked as if a giant had come along and whacked the buildings off about waist high, except a lone church. Germany was laid waste.

The plane full of men landed in Lyon, France. A representative from the Red Cross was there. No one had notified the Red Cross of the POW flights, and they were not ready for the number of POWs that would soon be in their care. All they had to feed the men at this point were dry cake donuts. Carl would have liked a nice hot cup of coffee to go with his donuts, but there was none. The men were strongly warned not to overeat. Their digestive systems were so weakened from starvation and bad food that it would take many months, and in some cases, years, before they worked normally again. One POW ate 17 donuts. When Carl saw the aftermath of that he felt bad about not trying to stop him. The food swelled up inside the man, and it was too much for him. The Germans had almost killed him; the donuts finished him off.

Once in France they were herded into a large cattle truck and taken to the train station. They then rode the train from there to Reims, France. Again they were picked up by trucks and headed back to Camp Lucky Strike. It was here the men would be debriefed about their Prisoner of War experience and be prepared to move back into society.

Forty thousand POWs arrived in this camp in a very short time. The camps were overwhelmed and understaffed, and not ready for the onslaught. The men piled off of the trucks anyway. The men were stripped and deloused, then allow to shower with a generous amount of warm water. Carl just stood under the water stream for a long time. Never before had a real shower felt so good. Then the men were allowed to pick through a bin of used fatigues uniforms, underwear and socks. Carl couldn't find a matching pair of socks but the two he got were clean!

One day shortly after he got to camp, Carl heard that Martin Stachoiwiak was in the hospital tent nearby. He immediately went to look for his right waist gunner. He asked the attendant to point him toward the correct cot, and went to find his friend and comrade, but when he looked down at the man in the bed, Carl was sure the attendant had directed him to the wrong man. He was about to turn and go back to ask the attendant again, when the shrunken skeletal man spoke his name. "Fyler. Its me." Carl recognized the voice, and turned to look again. He felt shocked as he looked at the ill and damaged man. Marty had a broken arm, been starved, bayoneted in both arms, and he had dog bites from where the Germans set the dogs on him, but he was alive! Carl sat down next to him, leaned forward with his elbows on his knees to hear him, and they began to talk.

Marty repeated the stories that Bill Addison had told Carl earlier about the horrendous conditions on the march from Stalag Luft 4. Marty finally managed to kill the red headed German who had been in charge of this horrific walk, then he and several others escaped and swam across a river to get to the Allied lines.

Marty also filled Carl in, first hand, about the details of tail gunner S/Sgt Joseph Sawicki's heroism in the back of the Dark Horse on that dark November day. Marty said that he had written Sawicki up for the Medal of Honor as soon as he reached Camp Lucky Strike. There was no doubt in Marty's mind that he and Fisher would have gone down with the plane and died without Sawicki's efforts to push them out of the plane. Marty also wrote Carl up for the Silver Star, as he had been so impressed with the way Carl stayed with the plane until the last minute to ensure that as many got out as was possible. Both sets of recommendations were apparently lost and never made it to the correct place.

At long last Carl felt fairly confident that he had a final accounting of all his crew. Of the 11 men, nine had bailed out, including him. Seven had been POWs. Two men, Sawicki and Ford, were killed in the plane. The only two he could not account for directly were Ray O'Connell and Nellins Egge the photographer, although he had heard that some German civilians had killed them on the ground. The gnawing in his gut began to subside.

The men had permission to go into Paris if they wished, but Carl had no desire to go there. He just wanted to go home. He missed Kansas, he missed his parents and his sister, and he missed his wife. Sometimes he missed it all so much it was an ache in his gut. So he spent his time writing and drawing and trying somehow, some way, to begin processing all that had happened to him since he had gone to England a year and a half before. It was a lot.

Other men were struggling with the aftermath of their brutal treatment as well. One day a GI went berserk and opened fired with his carbine near the Red Cross tent killing a number of GIs. It was going to be a long and difficult road for them all.

Carl was so ready to go home. At night his head would swim with all he needed to do. He worried about the finances, he worried about the situation between Ellen Jean and his mother, and he worried about what he would do to support his wife after he got home. So much to think about …

V-Mail, Monday May 21, 1945

Been a couple of days since I got out of Germany. I've written home when I was in Germany, it was so hard then, and now it is so easy, but I find it hard to find anything to write about. I have sent several cables to let you know I was okay, I hope you got them.

Now I am eating lots of good food! Will be fat as a pig if I don't eat myself to death first. I can't help it though; Good food is something a guy can't pass by after eating black brot and spoiled horsemeat for a year and a half …

I will get 60 days leave this summer sometime. I will be home, perhaps real soon, so look for me when I walk in the front door. See if dad can get 2 weeks off, same with EJ and perhaps we'll all go out and have a big bang! Should be a lot of fun!

Tell EJ to have bank reports and bonds up to date for me, as it is very important.

The Negro quartermaster troops are taking pretty good care of me; at least they feed me really good. So I can't complain except that I would really like to just get home. I get a shower every day, and clean clothes, which seems almost like a dream after Germany …

As always,
Carl

V-mail, June 5, 1945
Dear Mother, Dad, Gloria and Ellen,
Hello! Just a few lines as I am in a hurry. I am OK. I am feeling pretty fair. I have been eating good here, getting real fat again. I have put back on 20 of the 47 pounds I had lost. I plan to be home by the end of June, or this summer sometime. Plan to feed me a lot – tons of fresh vegetables, spinach, asparagus tips, etc., as well as fruit. I will get 60 days leave, or there abouts.

Tell EJ to have every record of papers of every sort ready for me to check! Bank accounts, checks, bonds, stuff from England and my old outfit, every little bit of account since I came overseas 2 years ago. I must have them to check! My future plans depend a lot on that.

Gloria should be through school by now. I hope she does OK. Marty and Addison went home via England but I did not as I was so eager to get home. Look for me when I get there.

As Always,
Carl

At long last the day came when Carl boarded the boat to get home ...

The ship that took Carl home was not the flagship of the fleet. There were still German submarines in the Atlantic, so the 5-inch gun crew practiced every day. The boat broke down in mid-trip, leaving them exposed like sitting ducks until repairs could be made. At one point the USS Constitution passed by them at full steam ahead, waving as they passed. The rundown little boat was overcrowded. The GIs had to sleep in shifts, as there were 12 officers in each small stateroom. The rest of the time they were out on deck.

The ship had a strangely mixed crew. The gun crew was US Navy. The engine room was staffed with Russians. The deck officers were Merchant Marines, and the captain had previously been a Mississippi riverboat captain.

At long last the ship limped into Newport News, Virginia. There was an Army band playing music. Some men came off the gangplanks and went down to the ground, kissing the earth of their homeland. Carl had rather hoped to go into New York City and to see the Statue of Liberty as he came home. He was disappointed to land in Virginia, but it was good to be home.

The newly returned men then boarded a Baltimore and Ohio train bound for Ft. Leavenworth, Kansas. The coach was an 1890s-style long, wooden car that sagged in the middle. Often the train pulled off onto sidings to let freight trains go by. It was an odd situation. There was no food for the men on the train. People in the little river towns would come out and wave to them. When they discovered the men had no food they would run home and bring back whatever food they had. They brought sandwiches of homemade bread, grapes, apples and such, and passed them through the open windows of the rail car into the outstretched hands of the men on the train. Such hospitality and kindness. It was much appreciated. These were Americans. It was so good to be back with his own people.

Finally the train reached Ft. Leavenworth in eastern Kansas. As the men disembarked they were handed $75 in pay. From there Carl went to Kansas City, Missouri and had some farewell drinks with his fellow ex-POWs at the Union train station. He then boarded a Santa Fe train to head toward Hutchinson, Kansas and home. It was a strange mix of feelings he had as he rode that train ... relief, fatigue, anxiety, happiness and dread. He was a changed person. He would never look at the world or at life the same way as he did the last time he was in Hutchinson. Would he ever really fit back into that world again after the things he had seen and experienced? Only time would tell. Mostly he was just excited to be going home! As a consequence of this anticipation, Carl spent most of the trip in the men's room.

The closer the train got to Hutchison, the more it seemed to slow. He had waited for this moment for so long, dreamed of it time and time again in the cold nights at Stalag Luft 1. He had pictured the scene ... the town gathered at the station, the band playing, Ellen Jean flying into his arms as his parents and his sister looked on ...

It wasn't like that at all when the train pulled into the station. The station was quiet. There was no band. All Carl saw standing on the platform were his mother, his father and his sister. The expressions on their faces filled him with alarm. Rushing out to them, he asked, "Where is Ellen Jean?"

John Fyler had dreaded this moment, because he knew his next words would break his son's already wounded heart. He put his hands on Carl's shoulder and said, "Son, she's gone. There is no point in going to her apartment, she's gone, we don't know where. So come on home with us son, and we'll decide what to do from here."

Carl felt as if he had been kicked hard in the stomach. He was stunned. Dumbfounded, he followed his parents to their car. They drove in silence to their comfortable little home.

As they sat around the living room later, the story came out about Ellen Jean. Carl heard how Ellen Jean had taken his monthly allotment checks, driven his car, and spent his savings. His parents told him that she had been true to him, to the best of their knowledge, until about two months before he returned, when she began to party and drink and how she had been seeing a married sailor. Carl sat there with $11 in his pocket, now all the money he had to his name. It all seemed like a bad dream. He couldn't believe what he was hearing. He was reeling. No, his first night at home was not at all how he had imagined it would be.

The next day Carl began to try frantically to get in touch with Ellen Jean. He wanted to understand, he wanted to know what had happened. He called his mother-in-law. He had always gotten along with her, he was sure she would help him. But she was cold and short with him, saying that Ellen Jean was in no condition to talk to him. Carl was stunned. How could someone not be in the condition to talk to her husband who had just gotten home from the war? Carl wrote to Ellen Jean and begged her to come back home and talk to him, to tell him what had happened. No word came, although rumors abounded around town, rumors of parties and men. Carl was despondent.

I spent some time down on the creek fishing. I needed to get my mind together and make some decisions for my future. I felt like a square peg in a round hole. I spoke half German and half English. If a car backfired I found myself on the ground trying to dig a foxhole and crawl into it. I had been through too much war. I had spent four years learning the meaning of death while I was still a youth. I had seen the face of terror, felt the stinging cold of fear, and had lived the reality of war and prison. I had lost my youth. I would never be the same. And now, betrayal. No one would ever know how deeply Ellen Jean had hurt me.

Finally, after weeks of silence, a letter came from Ellen Jean.

July 2, 1945, Yates Center, KS.

Dear Carl,
I don't know whether you deserve any note from me or not, but I will try to be a little fair with you anyway.

I went to that "guard house" you left me in unwillingly, because I thought I could do anything for you, but I guess any human being can be hurt beyond endurance. The truth has been forced upon me that you asked me to suffer what I have gone through. You knew your mother despised me and the family I came from, yet you demanded that I stay there. I realize how true is the saying, "I could not love thee half so much, loved I not honor more." For by going to live with someone who has insulted my family and me, my honor is at stake. And honesty and fairness are included in my family's standards. Carl, I do not mention insults and lies without proof and witnesses. Yes, you might be shocked at the multitude of them. No, I can't come there. Your father told me to leave and struck me with the paper he had in his hand. He threw me out! I was just going to pack my things to leave anyway because I had just been unbearably insulted and humiliated on the street before my friends by your mother. Your father rushed out and took my car keys and I knew he would get all my money too, if he could, hence the reason you find no checking account there.

You have been giving the orders. Well, Ellen is making up her own mind from now on. (Someone should be interested in her welfare.) On no condition whatever will I ever have anything to do with your folks ever again.

A few things that hurt:
1. Numerous reminders from your mother that my diamond ring belonged to her. Anything she ever did for me was thrown up to me.
2. Her saying I just wanted to be a war bride and that I just married you for your money. Carl, I know you know that at one time I loved you so much it hurt.
3. Your mother saying that after she told you at Phoenix my mother had treated her shamefully, you wanted to call off the wedding and pack mother and I both up and send us home. True?
4. You told me to try it for three months at your folks and if I wasn't happy to go home. But when you got away you gave me orders not to go home and not to visit in my own sister's home. I have just recently told the folks about this and it hurt, for they have been rather proud of you.

5. Your mother and father criticized me and accused me of not caring anything about you nearly every time I enjoyed myself with anyone except them.

This is only a little outline and surely you understand now why I am home instead of there where you left me.

So Carl it is rather tragic, after all you have been through, to come home to such "a harvest," but how could you expect consideration and respect if "no seeds have been sown?"

This is the most difficult letter I have ever written and out of fairness to you, I will listen to anything you have to say.

Ellen Jean Fyler

PS—I am sending along a package with gas stamps, bonds and other papers.

Then, on July 6, 1945, Carl was served with the divorce papers. And the reason for the divorce? Extreme cruelty. Carl laughed bitterly when he read that. "I have been gone for two years and I have been cruel to her?"

The divorce was granted. The judge pronounced it so, as Ellen Jean sat there next to her mother, smiling.

The war in the European Theater was over, but the war raged on in the Pacific the rest of the summer of 1945. Finally, on August 6 and 9, 1945, the first atomic bombs were dropped on Hiroshima and Nagasaki, Japan. Japan surrendered on August 15, 1945, and World War II was over.

Ellen Jean wrote Carl again on that day.

Dear Carl,
The war is over! It doesn't seem possible as it is hard to remember when there was no war, but I imagine we will all get back into the

groove again soon. For the last six years my life has been centered around you. Consequently it is hard for me to adjust myself to a different life. I know I can do it so I am not worried ...

I have written several letters to you but after reading them over I tore them up. Since I feel that I did the best I could while you were gone, I feel there is no more explanation necessary. I realize now that you must hate me, but after finding out you had a lawyer, I knew I could do nothing else toward bringing us back together. I hope you will be happy with your folks, as I know they are very glad to have you home again. I only hope you do not let your mother's imagination fool you as long as it did me. I feel only pity and not hate toward your folks.

I realize now that you did not love me enough when we were married and that I should have faced a few facts then, but I loved you so much I guess I was afraid of what those facts might be. Someday you will meet somebody that you will love more than anything in the world and I hope she will make you very happy because you have had so little happiness in your life. I wish I could have been the one though.

Carl, did I happen to leave a few dresses there in the cedar chest? I would like to have them. I found a few more odds and ends of yours that I am sending to you.

A fortuneteller with cards told me this was all going to happen quite some time ago. She said that you were going to learn a lesson from it. My lawyer didn't think you would. I wonder which one will be right?

Ellen Jean

What Ellen Jean did not know as she wrote the letter on that momentous day, was that she and the fortuneteller were both right.

The summer of 1945 was not an easy one for Carl Fyler. His body and mind were still trying to recoup from the abuse they took as a result of the war, and his heart needed healing as well. Fate had dealt him a hard blow, and for a while he was very bitter about life.

But Carl's friends and family gathered around him at this time. People reached out to him. One of the people who reached out to him was his pastor from his church in Spearville, A.P. Barnett. Carl had been saddened to learn that Rev. Barnett's son had been killed in the war, and Carl had written to the Reverend to express his condolences and to tell him of his own problems. A letter came in reply:

Dear Carl,

Thank you for your comforting words regarding my son. Of course his loss is a great sorrow to me. But the kind words and kind sympathy of his and my many friends help a lot.

Thanks too Carl, for your frank statement about your own troubles. Of course I had heard rumors but I didn't believe all I had heard. I have known you and your family too long and too intimately to accept some of the things reported. You surely have my sincere sympathy and my earnest hope you will be able to rise above this experience and carry on as a real Christian in the world. Don't let this embitter you or turn you against the best things in life. You have a high tradition to uphold in your fine family. Please give them my personal regards and best wishes. I hope all are better by now.

I have not been well at all since the first of the year until I went to Mayo Clinic and had an operation. But for the last six weeks I am very much better. I have resigned from the church in Spearville but I am going out there to do another service with them Sunday and to remove my things over here next week.

Thank you again for your letter Carl. Think and pray about what I have said. I will always be glad to hear from you any time.

Cordially, your friend

A.P Barnett

Carl sat still on the porch with the letter on his lap, considering his pastor's words. It occurred to him he really had two choices. One was to let the anger and the bitterness eat him alive, and cause him to turn to drink, as many of his fellow soldiers would, or he could learn something from the experience, and as the pastor said, choose the best things in life. He did have the Fyler tradition to uphold. He would be damned if he would let Ellen Jean and her shenanigans or the Germans get the best of him. He had to get on with his life. Carl had been considering going to dental school. His grandfather had been a dentist, and that was a career he could do even if he never did regain full function in his damaged leg and back. He liked the idea of being a professional man. As he sat on the porch that hot summer night, he made up his mind. He would begin investigating what it took to go to Dental School.

Besides, that pretty little blonde who worked at the post office was on his mind. His mother had reminded him of her. "That little blonde, Marguerite – you know, you saw a couple of times before you went to war – still works at the post office on the second floor." Helen wanted Carl to know there were other fish in the sea. He took notice.

One day shortly after that Carl found that he had some business to conduct at the post office. After he mailed his letter he went upstairs. "Sure enough, there she was, and just like that I was hooked." Carl and Marguerite began to seriously date.

In late summer, Carl was sent to a clinic in Miami Beach, Florida, for several weeks of evaluation, rest and rehabilitation. Before the war Carl would have really enjoyed the sights and sounds of Miami Beach, but as it was, he was having trouble enjoying his surroundings. He wrote home, saying:

Gloria would have really enjoyed the sights at Miami Beach. All those ritzy hotels, beautiful buildings, beaches, pools, good swimming, boating, fishing, dancing, seafood, well everything. The music was good, the kind of singing she hopes to do someday. She would have had a swell time dancing on the terrace by the ocean at night. I did not. I just enjoyed the good bed and three swims a day in the ocean.

I got a swell letter from Marguerite yesterday. She told me that you and Gloria had telephoned her. Thanks for giving her this address when you phoned her because it meant such a wonderful letter for me!

Mother, right now Marguerite is my ideal. In her letter she said that 15% of the men like blondes, said that I must be funny to be in that 15% as I must like what other people do not care for. But Mother, you said, "I think she is sweet," and now you have me believing it too!

I got the book about dreams you sent me. It says that jumping means success – do you remember I had that dream where I jumped off a ladder that Marguerite held. Remember the other dream I had where I saw Marguerite's face, just her face, against a black velvet background? The book says if you see just a face, and the face smiles, you will fall in love with that person ... and she smiled! I think I have fallen in love with her.

I asked Dr. Perry, my old bomb group field surgeon, about a career in Dentistry. He said it would be a good deal for me at 24 years old. He says to go and get it! I could make a good living at it according to him. So, I think I will do that, perhaps next summer or fall. Uncle Sam will pay for 4 years on the GI Bill!

There is not much more to write for now, so, so long, Please keep talking to Marguerite.

Always, Carl

Originally Carl had been scheduled to go back to war. He had been told he would go to Pilot Refresher School, then back to fight the Japanese. Carl had had enough. He really didn't want to go, although he was a soldier and would have gone and done his best if he had to do so. As always it was country first. However, the atomic bomb was dropped and the war was over. It was decided at that time that Carl would be honorably discharged from the military.

In late December, General Eisenhower promoted Carl to Captain. The paperwork for the original promotion that the German Interrogation officer had told Carl about had been lost in the shuffle of the war. Although Carl didn't know it, he had also been awarded the Distinguished Flying Cross decoration at that time as well. That fact was also lost. These errors would not be corrected until nearly 40 years later, in July 1982, when Carl would receive both his captain's bars and his medal. Therefore, the promotion given by General Eisenhower would be automatically moved up to the grade of major.

By now, Carl was a man in love. Marguerite was a petite woman with blonde hair, hazel eyes and a cute figure. She loved being a woman. She loved clothes and makeup and nail polish and hats. She looked like a movie star. She wasn't extravagant though. She could take everyday things and make them look like they came straight from Hollywood. She was sweet and always thought of others and how they might be feeling about things – sometimes even to the point of putting her own wishes on the shelf too much. She was dedicated and loyal once she made up her mind to commit to something or someone. She was a happy person and she had an inner light that shone from her such that she lit up a room just by walking into it. In general, Carl seldom thought about anything anymore but Marguerite and the life he wanted to have with her. Helen and John Fyler, and Marguerite's parents grew more and more concerned. They saw nothing wrong with the relationship but it was all happening so fast. Carl had been home such a short time; he had had such a short time to process all the hits he had taken. The parents cautioned them to slow down, to take their time, to wait until they knew for sure. But Carl Fyler knew exactly what he wanted by Christmas of 1945. He wanted to make Marguerite his wife. Marguerite also knew exactly what she wanted. When Carl Fyler asked her to marry him, she didn't think twice. She said yes.

1946

By the end of 1945, Carl had made the decision that he was indeed going to go to dental school, and he had chosen the Dental College in Kansas City, Missouri. However in working with the admission counselor at the school, he learned that he needed to have a few more college credits in science and math before he would be admitted to the school. In order to pick up those credits he had decided to enroll for the spring semester of 1946 at Bethany College in Lindsborg, Kansas. Gloria was working as a music teacher in Lindsborg and had an apartment there, so he could save expenses and live with her while going to school. It was all arranged and Carl moved to the tiny Swedish college town. He and Marguerite kept in touch by letter.

The couple had decided to set the date for the wedding as Feb. 14, 1946. Marguerite's mother in particular was very upset with this decision and let Margaret know in no uncertain terms that she would not give the marriage her blessing. Marguerite had left her mother's house in tears one late January afternoon. Carl, who was struggling with his college classes as well, wondered for a while if anything would go his way ever again. Then in early February he received another letter from Marguerite

Carl dear,
Things have been moving so fast here I hardly know where to begin to tell you but here goes.

As you know I had about reached the end of my rope on Sunday night. Yesterday your mother called me. She said she had been so worried about me all night that she could hardly sleep. We talked things over and she said for me to go home and discuss it all with Mom and come to a final decision. After supper last night Mom walked over to me and put her arms around me and said she loved me so much and she was never never going to hurt me again. She said she didn't know why she had acted as she did and hurt me so unless it was because it was jealousy and fear of losing me. She said she was going to die if she didn't snap out of it and she was going to try. She said my Dad has stayed loyal to me through it all anyway. She said if we want to be married on the 14th it was all right with her and she would do whatever I wanted her to do and that we could all plan it together.

Well how's this? I know you probably don't want to know but I really think it's best. We are going to have the wedding at my home with my minister. Your mother said yesterday noon when I talked to her that you would be willing to do it that way if I thought it was best so I am hoping you will agree. Mother sort of wants my aunts and uncles and grandparents there so we are going to be quite a few people after all. I didn't really want that many but I guess it will be OK. I think we will arrange candles in front of the fireplace and I will have Geneva light them. I may have someone sing. Would Gloria like to sing or would she rather be bridesmaid? She would probably rather be bridesmaid wouldn't she? I would love to have her be my bridesmaid. We can get a lot of these things planned out definitely over the weekend. We are going to serve cake and coffee afterwards. I think I will have Willa and Geneva help serve. There will be about 25 there unless you have someone else you want to be there. Then there will be more. Mother said we could arrange chairs in front and around the divan. There are so many things that need to be planned or worked out but at least I have a start and I HAVE MY PARENTS' CONSENT!

I know Mother still doesn't really approve and she thinks I am being a little hasty in getting married so soon, but she is going to make an effort to be more kind and we must help her all we can Carl. I know she isn't doing it just to "save her neck" because I could really talk to her last night for the first time in months. We could discuss things without getting mad or saying the wrong things. I really think she thought we might put it off a little longer if she gave her approval but I know it is best to go ahead and do it now and she will settle down and get over it that much quicker.

We mustn't forget to get reservations for the honeymoon at the Broadmoor Hotel in Wichita. I am going to get some film for the camera. I *do wish we could find an apartment in Lindsborg this weekend so I could get some of my things moved in. Do you think if we can't find one this weekend that it might be best to rent a room so we will have it and then look for an apartment? I really don't know, whatever you think is best.*

If any of these plans don't suit you darling then give me some of your own because after all both of us have to be pleased you know.

Darling, I know we are going to be so happy and have such a good life together. As I told your Mother yesterday just being with you is enough – I don't always have to be doing things to be happy and she said she knew that was true. She said she knew I could make you far happier than you have been and that she and your dad thought it was OK to get married now instead of waiting. She said she knew we would both be more content. I only hope I don't ever ever disappoint her or you either.

Well, I must go get some work done. I will see you Thursday or Friday, plan for a very busy weekend,

*All my love,
Marguerite*

The wedding did take place on that cold February day, with their family and friends gathered around in the Burris family living room. Despite their families' fears, it was a union that would last for 63 years, and a love that would last

forever.

The Good Life

After successful completion of his classes at Bethany, Carl was accepted into the dental school in Kansas City. The couple rented a nice little house, the perfect spot to set up housekeeping, and set out to enjoy their married life.

The bookwork part of school had always been hard for Carl's three-dimensional mind, but the practical part, the labs on human anatomy and building teeth were things that greatly interested him. He threw himself into his studies with great fervor. He wanted to be a good provider for his wife and to do something that was helpful to others. He wanted his family to be proud of him. And so he worked as hard as he could to do well in school. Marguerite was happy in her new little house. They were deeply in love, and though they were not wealthy with material things, they were wealthy in the things that mattered. Carl sighed a contented sigh as he remembered those early days. Even at the time, it had seemed strange to him that he could be so despondent in one year, and so happy and fulfilled in the next. But that was how it was, and soon they begin to build the life they had dreamed of living together.

One day Carl met a retired dentist, and the two began to talk. The elderly dentist told Carl that he and his beautiful wife should live life to the fullest, to travel and meet new people and experience new things while they could, because you never knew what life would bring. The dentist and his wife had put everything off until "later," when they were out of school and then after their kids were grown, and when later finally came his wife up and died. "Don't make that mistake boy," the old dentist told him, "live life while you can." Carl thought of how quickly in his own life his fortunes had gone from good to bad to very bad to good again, and he knew the man was right. Carl took the advice to heart. So he and Marguerite began right away to take trips. They enjoyed just packing up the car and heading off somewhere to see the sights. They frequently took family with them – their parents, Marguerite's younger sister, or Gloria and her new husband, a handsome Marine named Jack. Carl loved to take photographs, and Marguerite carefully preserved these photographic memories in a nice scrapbook her mother had given her. The war had taught them the hard lesson that sometimes, people and things you loved went away forever. This way, Marguerite could hold the good memories banked in her heart, ready to remember by opening the book and seeing the smiling faces.

Together Carl and Marguerite made it through dental school. As the May of 1951 graduation neared, the two of them sat down and looked at where they wanted to set up practice. The capital city of Kansas seemed the spot.

Topeka, Kansas, was an up and coming place in 1951. As the state capital it benefited from all the job positions needed to run the state government. The Menninger Clinic, founded in 1919, had become the premier location for psychiatric services, treatment and training for the newly developed field of psychiatry. There was a large Veterans Administration hospital in Topeka, founded in 1942. Security Benefit was a prospering insurance company, one of several headquartered in

Topeka. Of course Topeka was also the home office of the Atchison, Topeka and the Santa Fe railroad. In short, Topeka seemed to be a growing city that was going to need a good dentist, and Carl Fyler would fit that bill.

Soon he had set up shop on Kansas Avenue in downtown Topeka, and the patients came soon after. He and Marguerite bought a cute little cottage in central Topeka, and settled down to their new life as Dr. and Mrs. Carl J. Fyler.

It quickly became apparent that while Carl was a good dentist, bookkeeping was not his strong point. Marguerite however, had a head for numbers, and so it came to be that Marguerite was the office manager for Carl's dental practice. It was a team that worked well. Patients grew to love being greeted by Marguerite's smiling face. They knew Doctor Fyler would take time with them, tell them stories, and make them laugh. Many of the patients became friends. The practice grew, and life was good.

However a setback occurred on June 8, 1966, when a huge tornado cut a mile-long diagonal swath across the city of Topeka. Carl's office in the National Reserve Life building took a direct hit from the storm. The building's shell stood, but all its windows and its entire contents were sucked out into Kansas Avenue. When Carl and Marguerite were finally allowed into the downtown area, they stood ankle deep in the debris, a sick feeling in their stomachs. Ironically, the huge sign on the side of the building stood, still intact, reading "National Reserve Life: A Refuge in Time of Storm." At first they were told

that the building was going to be razed, as there were fears it was no longer structurally sound. Later the engineers determined that this was not the case, and the building still stands today at the corner of 10th and Kansas. By that time Carl and Marguerite had picked up, cleaned up and moved a block up the street to the Mills Building at Ninth and Kansas. They started over with the dental practice, and the patients followed.

Carl's love for flying had not abated after the war. One day a patient told him about a man who had an old airplane for sale. It was not in flying condition. The man had it stored in a barn, and the patient said he knew the man would sell it cheap. Carl knew at that moment that he would buy the plane, and he just hoped Marguerite would go along with it.

He went to see the plane. There in the dusty shadows of the old barn she sat, looking forlorn and abandoned. Carl's heart skipped a beat. It was just like the one he had learned to fly in back before the war! That seemed so long ago now. Carl walked around the plane, his mind working over how he could rebuild her and make her airworthy again. He looked up and asked how much. Before he left the barn, Carl Fyler was the proud owner of a used airplane, but he was as

thrilled as if she had just come off of the line all shiny and new. Carl hooked the plane to the bumper of his car and dragged it to a small airfield near his house. There Carl labored over the plane after work and on weekends, until at last she could fly. As Carl taxied up the field after her maiden flight, he was ecstatic.

Carl never forgot his first plane. He even kept her prop as a memento. Which one of his nephews had that prop now? One of them did. He just couldn't remember which one at the moment. She would be the first of several planes he would own, but she was the only one he refurbished himself. Carl had many adventures with his planes! Once he was testing out a new plane. The drawback in test piloting a new plane is by the time a problem is located there might be trouble! As Carl came to the end of the runway on takeoff, the plane suddenly lost power. He pulled the nose up, but she wasn't going to fly. Instead the plane flipped over. The people in the tower raced to the scene. There was Carl, hanging upside down in the harness, unhurt. Later someone asked him if he had been afraid. Honestly, after that day in November of 1943, it was pretty hard for him to be afraid of much in an airplane, but he had been afraid … of what Marguerite would say to him when she learned he had just crashed his brand new plane!

Besides airplanes, Carl had another hobby – rock hunting. He had always loved looking for interesting rocks and arrowheads. This interest had ignited into a real passion. So Carl combined all his joys: his wife, flying, traveling, rock and treasure hunting. He pursued life with gusto, traveling the world.

The memory stayed in his mind like a lovely little melody. He saw the plane land lithely on the grassy strip and taxi over to park. They gathered their cameras, hiking gear and their lunch, and climbed out. Carl remembered feeling as excited as a kid at the circus for the first time. He was living out the great adventures he had always read about as a youth … swashbuckling characters with the beautiful woman on their arms, searching for treasure. Ruby, amethyst, lapis … all the stones coveted for their beauty in jewelry. Carl began to read voraciously about rocks and minerals and soon was quite knowledgeable. He also knew where and how to search for arrowheads and meteorites. He knew that what looked like a plain rock to many actually was more valuable than the gemstones he found. He easily recognized that rusty black rock

had been in outer space before making a fiery plunge to the earth's surface. All these things fascinated him. Carl always wrote to obtain permission to go on the lands he entered, and seldom met with any opposition. So he and Marguerite hiked and explored and hunted treasure to their hearts' content. They explored all the national parks, off the tourist roads. Carl recalled that day, one of many such days, with exquisite detail. He saw himself sitting on a rock near a crystal clear stream in Rocky Mountain National park with Marguerite at his side, hand in hand. He remembered thinking about the war years, then some 10 years past. At that moment those difficult days seemed like a bad dream he had once upon a time. He looked at Marguerite. The sun was warm and glistening on her hair. She looked up at him and smiled. He now couldn't be happier.

****

The dental practice continued to grow and soon Carl and Marguerite were doing well for themselves. Carl had become active in the Dental Association and he and Marguerite traveled all over the world going to meetings of various groups and going on cruises. Carl never forgot the words of that old dentist. He intended to live life to its fullest.

They never had children. Marguerite would later tell someone that she felt Carl needed all of her attention that would be divided if children came along. There were plenty of nieces and nephews to go around anyway.

Carl decided it would be fun to have a cabin. He wanted one that was in the woods, next to a lake where he could go to fish and hunt and enjoy the great outdoors. He began to ask around. It wasn't long before he found the perfect one. It was a log cabin nestled in the woods that grew around Mission Creek near Dover, Kansas. The area had been a favorite camping ground for the Indians in days past, and Carl found it to be a treasure trove for arrowheads. There was a low water dam across the creek, creating behind it a beautiful pool, perfect for fishing, just up the trail from the cabin. Carl loved to take his nephews to the pool to fish. One day his sister's youngest, Kirby, then aged 5, slipped off the dam and went under! It was only because of Gloria's quick reaction time and sturdy belt loops on his shorts that he survived the ordeal! They had an old dog at that time that loved

to go down and fish as well. The dog would herd the children back if they wandered too far away from the cabin.

Carl often went back to that beautiful spot in his mind. Oh, the good times there, lots of good drink and good food, cooking fish or steaks. His mouth watered as he remembered a time when he could actually eat and enjoy a meal. If only he could go there again, roll back time. Idyllic memories flooded through him, like Mission Lake after a big rainstorm …

It was indeed a good life after all.

More Battles to Fight

Even though things were going well, there were some concerns. Carl continued to struggle with the aftermath of war. He frequently had trouble sleeping due to nightmares. Things would trigger his memories. He relived the crash of the Dark Horse in his mind so many times that he lost count. His digestion never really did return to normal. In addition, Carl had completely lost the mobility of his left leg, the consequences of being hit by a jeep, wounded by shrapnel, sliding down a 60-foot pine tree, and no medical care for the resulting severe injuries. As Carl talked to fellow veterans, he learned that they too were experiencing such things. It also became apparent very quickly that although the Veteran's Administration was supposed to be there to assist veterans, that help was hard to come by.
Ex-Pisoners of War, in particular, were in need of assistance.

"The starvation, exposure to the elements and other things encountered by the Prisoner of War would quickly prove to cause long-term damage to vital organs. Former Prisoners of War are

eligible for special veterans benefits, including medical care in VA hospitals and disability compensation for injuries and diseases caused by internment. These benefits are in addition to regular veterans benefits and services to which they, as veterans, are entitled."
(American Ex POWS)

The problem seemed to be that the VA kept forgetting that the ex-POWs were entitled to these benefits. In the first place, the VA made it very hard for anyone to qualify for benefits. In order to qualify to have 100% coverage, by the way the VA calculated things, a person would need to prove he or she was 150% disabled by his POW experience. At length Carl himself was determined to be 100% disabled, yet every time he had a medical claim he would receive a bill for those services, and he would have to go in and prove all over again that the VA themselves had determined he was 100% disabled. He was denied over and over again. Since Carl was being refused his own entitled benefits he knew other POWs were experiencing the same treatment.

And thus began the battle.

The heartlessness shown by the VA to those who had served their country incensed Carl. He became determined he would take on the system and win. He set up a command center in the back part of his house, and began fighting for others as he battled for himself, filling out paperwork, doing research, and helping many veterans from all branches of the service and from all wars and conflicts to obtain the services and benefits to which they were entitled. This was all done without benefit of computers or the Internet. Carl's weapons were paper and pen, stamps and envelopes, telephone and copy machine, and dogged perseverance. He frequented Capital Hill in Washington, D.C., and was well known at the Kansas State House as he fought for laws to protect veterans. He served in various capacities in Veteran's Rights groups. He helped to found a Kansas Ex-POW Chapter, and served as its president for many years. He also served with the National Chapter as well.

Carl even got Prisoner of War license plates authorized by the state of Kansas. He was proud of the day he stood with the Governor as he signed the bill. In short time he was considered to be the national expert on ex-POW affairs. Carl continued this battle until he could fight no more. He then passed the baton to others in his Ex-POW group, giving them instructions on to carry on in his stead. He never gave up.

Carl was fighting another battle, one that had started on November 29, 1943, and did not end until the day he died. This battle was the one to award S/Sgt. Joseph R. Sawicki the honor that he had earned. From the beginning Carl was impressed with that young man, so fearless even then. He had been pleased to have him join the crew when Jillson moved on to HQ. When Carl heard about Sawicki's actions in the tail of the Dark Horse on that fateful day, he knew that he would make sure that Sawicki's sacrifice would not go unnoticed. As soon as he was out of Stalag Luft 1, while at Camp Lucky Strike, he had filled out the paperwork to get Sawicki the Congressional Medal of Honor, as did Martin Stachowiak.

The Congressional Medal of Honor is the highest military decoration awarded by the United States. The decoration is bestowed on members of the United States Armed Forces who distinguish themselves through "conspicuous gallantry and intrepidity at the risk of his or her life above and beyond the call of duty while engaged in an action against an enemy of the United States. It is often bestowed posthumously.

Members of all branches of the armed forces are eligible to receive the medal. The Medal of Honor is bestowed upon an individual by the passing of a Joint Resolution in the Congress; and is then personally presented to the recipient or, in the case of posthumous awards, to next of kin, by the President of the United States, on behalf of the Congress, representing and recognizing the gratitude of the American people as a whole. This seemed only appropriate to Carl.

However, the first paperwork he filled out and sent in from France never made it to the appropriate desk. Carl proceeded to fill the paperwork out again and again. Each time the paperwork was lost or he was given some reason why the award could not be granted. Carl's frustration grew with each excuse. He heard that the paperwork wasn't filled out in a timely fashion, that Sawicki hadn't killed any more enemy fighters with his actions, or that Carl did not witness the actions himself. Years later he got the excuse that "there were no first hand witnesses," or that there was "no family left to received the award." By that time, those statements were true.

Carl wrote every Congressional member he could think of. Finally, in the 1990s, the Senator from Kansas came very close to getting the apparent impossible accomplished. He managed to bring a bill before Congress. However, there was not enough support, and it failed. Carl's frustration and determination knew no end. He would make sure every one knew about the bravery of Joseph R. Sawicki. It was for this reason that he agreed to write his book, *"Staying Alive."* He would do anything he could to tell the world about Joseph.

Carl did not know it at first, but Joseph Sawicki's family was fighting their own battles. After receiving the devastating news that their only son was missing in action, they learned he had been killed in action, but no body could be found. Finally, the Army learned that the body had been found by the Germans in the wreckage of the plane just north of Bremen, and buried in a nearby POW cemetery. Later, the body was exhumed and moved to a military cemetery in Belgium. At long last, Tilly and Joseph Sawicki Sr. were able to bring their beloved son home. He is buried in the family plot near Detroit, Michigan today. But the family got little else of their son's belongings back.

In a letter written in 1944, Joseph Sr. wrote:

We received the box with the clothing items, but my son's uniforms were not among those items. We are especially anxious to have his uniforms. Would you please let us know how to go about making inquires about his uniforms?

Thank you in advance for your kindness in taking care of this matter.
Sincerely,
Joseph P. Sawicki

In a later letter dated March 19, 1947, Joseph's mother Tillie wrote:

We have never received back any of our son's personal belongings. We filed a claim a long time ago and were informed that nothing has been found that belonged to our son Joseph. And yet we knew that he had a lot of things and gifts for his family, as he was expecting to come home. He was also saving his money for that purpose.

So please give this matter your earliest attention.

Hoping to hear from you at your earliest convenience.

Yours truly,
Tillie Sawicki

At length the sorrowing family received a note from the Office of the Quartermaster in Kansas City, Missouri, informing them that no personal effects of Joseph R. Sawicki were ever found, save for some pocket change. It was itemized out for them:

1 quarter
1 nickel
1 dime
1 penny

This is all the family would ever receive from the Army. Carl's heart ached for them when he learned of this in a letter from Mrs. Sawicki.

He could imagine her, holding the corroded coins in her hand, tears streaming down her face. It must have seemed to them that the price of her son's life, given for his country, was exactly 41 cents. That thought strengthened Carl's resolve to continue the fight, no matter what roadblocks were put in his way. Joseph R. Sawicki would not die in vain.

Endings

The time ticked away. At first, Carl thought his stay at the VA was going to be temporary. Marguerite's family had instructed the housekeeper to drop her off at a respite care facility, so for the moment at least she was safe, though desperately unhappy there without him. But as the days passed, Carl realized that for some unknown reason no efforts were being made to get them home or even for them to see each other. They depended on the telephone now as their only connection, but this was not very satisfactory, especially since they had both become hearing impaired. They did the best they could but they were miserable without each other. The time they got to speak to each other became more valuable to them than gold. To make matters worse, the staff at the VA began to say that he wasn't able to take care of himself or Marguerite any more, that they shouldn't live at home any more, and in fact that they should not even be together. He felt like there were some that wanted him to just sit in the VA and rot. All of this made Carl furious. He would get out of this place, but how could he get Marguerite home too? By God he would do it! He lay in bed, marking time and making plans …

Meanwhile, there were bills to be paid, a house to take care of, and business to conduct. Carl worried about how to accomplish these things. Finally, though full of reservations, he gave his bankbook to his housekeeper and asked her to deposit checks and pay bills. But when all of a sudden the housekeeper's phone was disconnected and he had no way to reach her, the camel's back broke. Carl was in a panic, trapped in a hospital bed tied to a tube that he needed to stay alive. What could he do? How did he wind up being separated from the love of his life? Something was horribly wrong. Somebody had to step in and help him resolve this travesty. Carl decided at last that he had no choice any more. He loved all his family, but it was Gloria's youngest son, Kirby, who he felt was most like him. He had never had a son of his own, but if someone came close it was this one. They thought alike. Carl smiled as he thought of all the hours they had spent on the phone talking politics and solving all the problems of the world. He knew whom he needed to call. Carl swallowed his pride and picked up the phone.

"Hello boy," Carl said as his nephew answered the phone. They talked a few moments as always of politics and world events, and then he dropped the bomb. He told his nephew about all that had happened, the problems with his eating and the VA; he laid out everything this time, holding nothing back. "I need some help. I need you to help Marguerite and I to get back together and to get back home. I also want you to be the executor of my will and my power of attorney. I am going to need some help now, and you are the one I trust to do it. Will help me boy?"

Kirby never hesitated. "I would be honored to help you in any way I can, " he replied.

"I appreciate that very much. But one thing you need to remember. "Ich bin Koenig."

"What does that mean?," Kirby asked.

"It means "I am King," in German."

"I guess that means I work for you."

"That's right boy. Don't ever forget that. You report to me."
"I understand that Carl."

"Good. I knew I could count on you. Now let's get busy."

The first task Kirby was faced with was how to get Carl and Marguerite back together again. He was shocked and appalled at how long they had been kept apart. He realized this would be no easy task. He did not know who or what was behind the lengthy separation, but he knew that something had to be done quickly to bring them back together in the same dwelling. In 62 years they had never been apart from each other and they needed to be together now more than ever. He wondered why Carl had never mentioned what was going on in the letters they had exchanged. It broke his heart to think of it. Kirby vowed to Carl that he would bring them back together, and he would, no matter what.

In the meantime Carl knew what he had to do. He had to get out of the VA hospital and back to his own home, where once again he could care for himself and Marguerite. He was becoming more and more certain that people were out to get him and his money. Some of his family had been asking questions that were alarming to him, prying into his personal business, telling him that he had to stay at the VA and sell his house. His outrage grew as he lay there. How dare they tell him how to live his life? He may have a bad leg and a bad throat, but he was still on top of his game.

At this point Carl and Marguerite decided it was time to make some important decisions. They discussed things thoroughly in their daily calls. They determined that they wanted to put Kirby in charge should they not be able to take care of things any more. He then made the necessary legal arrangements to ensure that would happen.

Carl decided at that point to be proactive. He knew his rights. No one could make him do what he didn't want to do. After all, he had helped so many in this situation in the past. He knew the laws. Carl went to the VA social worker and told her he wanted to set up a meeting. In this meeting he wanted to discuss their future and what steps they would have to take to return to their own home. Carl had always been reluctant to have people come in to help him with nursing care, and he didn't want to spend the kind of money he knew that would cost, but he was willing to make that compromise to go home. His nephew and his wife Heidi were working behind the scenes to accomplish just that. Most importantly, he wanted his wife of 60 plus years there for the meeting. After all, this big gathering was to decide their fate. Surely they had the right to be there together for that? He would resolve this once and for all. The social worker grudgingly agreed to schedule the meeting.

It was after his request to schedule a meeting that Carl's fears worsened. Many doctors came in to talk to him. It was almost like an interrogation! The doctors asked him all kinds of questions, but he still knew the answers! One doctor made the mistake of asking him who the President was, and Carl proceded to name all the Presidents, in order, with some political commentary on each. That doctor left the room with his tail between his legs! Carl realized that someone was using the system, trying to get him declared incompetent. But who would do such a thing? He also knew that they could not legally make him do anything as long as he could prove himself competent. Too bad for them he still had it!

Carl expressed to his nephew that it seemed that people were trying to keep him and Marguerite away from each other. The VA social worker also told him that the respite care center staff was saying that it would be too difficult for Marguerite to attend the meeting. Carl was outraged.

"She is my wife. We have made decisions together all these years. Nothing has changed. She still has her rights! Of course she must come to this meeting. It is to decide HER life after all! What are they thinking?!" He just couldn't believe what was happening. So he took it upon himself to make arrangements for Marguerite to be there.

The day of the meeting finally arrived.

Kirby and Heidi came to the meeting, along with his brother. The pastor and another woman from the church were there. His financial advisors were there. Marguerite's sister was there. His housekeeper was there. The social worker, doctors, aides, and the head of the home health agency were in attendance. Everyone was there but one person – the most important person.

Carl grew more and more agitated and alarmed as people filed in and took their place around the conference room table. Everyone was there, except Marguerite. Carl was so disappointed he didn't think he could take it. Where was she? He demanded to know what had happened. The woman from the church, with whom he had made arrangements to bring his wife to the meeting, said that she had been advised that the respite care center staff would not release Marguerite to come to the meeting. Carl was devastated. How could he face this meeting alone? How could he explain to them by himself that he and Marguerite just wanted to be left alone in their home. They had talked. If they were to die they wanted to die in their own home together. If it had been up to him, he would have called the whole thing off right then and there, even if his nephews had driven all the way from Tulsa to be there! The meeting took place anyway. Carl sat in stunned silence as they went around the table, one by one and each said they felt he needed to stay in the VA's long-term care facility, with Marguerite staying elsewhere.

When it came time for his nephew Kirby to speak, he looked Carl straight in the eye and said simply, "Carl, what do YOU want to do?"

Carl's face lit up. He smiled at his nephew. He stood up with the help of his cane and addressed the group with great dignity. It reminded Kirby of the scene in the movie Pearl Harbor when President Roosevelt stood up from his wheelchair and demanded that his advisors get the job done. Roosevelt's mission had been to bomb Tokyo. Carl simply wanted to go home. So Carl proposed that he and Marguerite return home, with home health care. He requested that they be allowed to live out the remainder of their days together in their own home. Then he sat back down, feeling deflated. He felt everyone had betrayed him except his family from Tulsa, and his church. He realized that these were the only ones who understood him and understood his wishes, right or wrong. There was no way he would ever agree to stay at the VA, with Marguerite elsewhere. They would not be separated. He would sign himself out of the VA if he had to do so. It was going to be a very difficult mission.

The meeting ended in a stalemate. Carl's family took him back to his room, where he was beside himself, literally shaking with frustration and anger at what had just happened.

'"Carl, look I don't know what happened," Kirby said. "I don't know why Marguerite wasn't here. But I will look into it. I will find out. And I will take you to see her. We will take you there ourselves. Tomorrow, no matter what."

"My god boy, do you realize I haven't been allowed to see my own wife since I was hospitalized in October, and it's FEBRUARY?! We have never been apart that long. Why is this happening, boy?"

"I don't know Carl, I don't know, but you should be able to visit your own wife. We will make that happen."

There seemed to be some conspiracy about keeping Carl and Marguerite apart. This incensed Kirby. The next day, they arrived at the VA to pick Carl up to take him to see his wife. When they walked up to the facility they saw Carl at the door in his wheelchair, grinning from ear to ear. In his hand was a card he had made for Marguerite. It was going to be a red-letter day for them.

When they got to the respite care center, the nephews hustled around and got Carl out of the van. They wheeled him up to the door and pushed the buzzer for admittance. A voice came over the intercom.

"May I help you?"

Heidi replied, "We are here to visit Marguerite Fyler."

There was silence for a second, then the voice said, "I am sorry, but there is no one here to let you in."

They all looked around in amazement, as the parking lot was full of cars. Kirby took hold of the wheel chair, spun Carl around and said, "Come on, we are going to see Marguerite come hell or high water. We will find another way in."

The group drove around to the back of the building and parked the van near another entrance, marked "For Employees Only."

"OK listen," Kirby said, "Here's the plan. Heidi and I are going to go in and scout out the place. We will find Marguerite, then come back to this door. One of us will stay inside to let the others in and the other one will come out and get you, Carl, and take you in. You two stay in the van and wait."

Carl was grinning by now. He was excited to see Marguerite and all the espionage seemed rather fun. Kirby and Heidi got out and walked up to the door. It was locked, but when Kirby reached up and pushed the buzzer the door immediately opened. As they strolled in, Kirby said to Heidi, "Listen, look for the youngest person you can find, someone who looks like they are too new to be in the loop, and ask them about Marguerite."

They found a young woman sitting at the desk. "Can I help you?" she asked politely.

"Yes, we are looking for Marguerite Fyler."

"Oh she is sitting right around the corner in the dining room, eating a bowl of cereal."

Sure enough there she was. So Kirby and Heidi went back to the employee entrance. On their way to the door, they encountered two nurses.

"Can we help you get someone in the building?" they asked.

"Oh that would be very nice," Kirby replied with a smile.

And so the two nurses actually brought Carl into the building with his family following behind. As Carl was wheeled around the corner Marguerite looked up and saw her husband.

"Carl! Is that you Carl? Oh Carl." she cried out in surprise.

She turned and spoke to the rest of the family. "You brought Carl to me! Do you know how long it has been since I have seen him?" she cried.

It was a joyous reunion. As the couple held hands and kissed and shed tears together Kirby took photographs of the occasion. He felt pleased and satisfied that he and Heidi had been able to bring about this reunion. The joy and love he saw as he watched his aunt and uncle was a beautiful sight to see. He could not understand why others could not see that no matter their age, these two were still humans who shared a great love and deserved to be able to determine their own destiny, together. There was no magic age at which people lost that right. Kirby sighed as he thought of all the times and places where those things were taken away from the elderly. It just shouldn't be.

Carl told Marguerite about the meeting.

"I don't know why they wouldn't let me go to the meeting Carl. I wanted to go. They told me I was going to go, but then yesterday they said I couldn't go."

"I tried to get you there," Carl said. "I called this facility and made arrangements and I got someone from the church to come over to pick you up. I don't know what happened either. But it's past now. What do you want to do Marguerite? Where do we go from here?"

"I want what you want Carl. I just want to be with you. That's all I need."

"We will make it so," he promised.

Marguerite took hold of Kirby's hand. "Thank you so much for getting us back together. You gotta get me out of here. Look at these people. All they do is sit here and stare. I don't know why I am still here. If I stay here any longer I will wind up like these people. I belong with Carl. Can you make sure we will be back together?"

"I will do whatever I can. It is paramount to me." She beamed a smile up at him and patted his hand.

After a hard goodbye, Carl's family took him back to his room at the VA, now lonelier after being in Marguerite's presence then it had been before. Heidi busied herself around the room, and Carl began to watch her and listen to her. He realized suddenly that his nephew had found himself a wife who was very much like Marguerite, one with a good heart and a good head, one who could organize details and take care of business. And so when she began to earnestly talk to him about the situation at hand, he listened.

"Carl, maybe what we need to do for now is just get you and Marguerite together," Heidi said. "You are too weak to be alone right now, with the tube in your stomach and all. What if we found a place where you could live together, just temporarily, until we can find a way to get you home?"

Carl considered what she had said. He felt like he had been betrayed by people he thought he could trust. He had had it with people who were trying to keep him and Marguerite apart, he was tired of people not respecting his independence, not treating him with dignity and respect. That being said, and for all his bravado, Carl was greatly alarmed at how weak he was becoming. He knew he needed help, and he knew he had been right in trusting Kirby and Heidi. In his heart, he knew Heidi was right. He also realized she had what it took to get everything done. And so, he reluctantly agreed to allow her to look for such a place.

"But you will get us home eventually?" he demanded of them.

"We will do everything in our power to get you there."

And they left it at that.

One afternoon before he left the VA, Carl decided to go to the house for a while. He needed to take care of some things, and besides that he just wanted to prove to others and to himself that he was capable of doing such a thing. However the outing did not go as well as he had hoped. Upon arrival at the house, as the cab drove off, he was so weak that he fell to the cold pavement on the driveway. He crawled up to the house with the help of his trusty cane, which he extended forward and used to pull himself along. Finally, he managed to get up and get himself in the door. Frightened by his own limitations and greatly out of breath, he called Kirby at work.

"I am at the house, boy. I fell in the driveway. I went AWOL by calling a cab, but as the cab left I fell in the driveway. I just crawled into the house, it took me an hour, but I did it. I didn't realize just how bad off I really am."

Kirby was alarmed, but he knew he had to be careful with how he handled this situation. He knew he had to respect his uncle's right to do what he wanted, and at the same time keep him safe. His mind was working like crazy to walk that tightrope.

"You need to call an ambulance Carl. You need to go back to the VA where you will be safe. You need to stay there and regain your strength while we figure out what to do. I told you I would help you get home and I will, but for now I need you to go back."

Carl realized the wisdom in his nephew's words, but he wasn't going to call an ambulance. So he called his trusted friend and neighbor, who came and took him back to the VA. He snuck in the back door. No one knew he had ever been gone but his legs felt like there were no bones in them, just rags. Carl was beginning to come to terms with just how ill he really was.

Kirby and Heidi made arrangements to have Carl transported over to see

Marguerite again the following week. It was February 14, 2009, Valentines Day, and their 63rd wedding anniversary.

Carl began to feel much less anxious about things. He knew his nephew and his wife would do what needed to be done. He knew they would take on the daunting long-distance tasks of ensuring that the bills were paid and the house taken care of. It was a great load off of his mind.

Kirby and Heidi made the arrangements for Carl and Marguerite to live together in a comfortable room at a retirement home. They came to Topeka and spent the weekend moving them into their new quarters. Carl felt exhausted from just watching them work. After his family said their goodbyes at the end of the weekend and headed back to Oklahoma, Carl sat back and looked around the room. It was one big room with a lovely bay window that allowed them to look out on the world. He and Marguerite each had their own comfortable recliners, and the walls were adorned with his sister's paintings. He gazed at the one on the wall across from his chair. It was one of their favorites, the one of the wooded path down to the cabin. He was glad to have that painting there. He could sit in his chair and remember the good times gone by. He hadn't wanted to come here. He had wanted to go home, but for now, this would do.

And so he came to be in the place where he would end his days, even though he did not know it at the time. Kirby and Heidi did make arrangements for him and Marguerite to go home with help, but when the time came he could not go. Carl had developed aspiration pneumonia. His lungs were slowly filling with fluid; fluid through which he could not breathe.

He was at the beginning of the end.

****

The activity director at the retirement home came to visit him every day. Carl really liked the man and looked forward to his visits. The man was a veteran too, and he and Carl had developed a mutual admiration society. When the director came to Carl and asked him if he would make a speech and be part of a program honoring veterans, Carl didn't hesitate to say yes, even though he knew he was growing weaker with each passing day. After the director left the room, anxious to begin planning for the event, Carl leaned back in his chair and thought about what he wanted to say. He called his neighbor and asked him to go to his house and bring his good jacket and some other items so that he could put together his presentation. He didn't know why, but for some reason this little speech seemed to hold great importance. It was to be his swan song.

A few days later, Carl stood up to tell his story of war at the podium. His legs were weak and shaky, but he would do this if it were the last thing he would ever do. He looked out in the room full of gray hair, walkers and wheelchairs. That's what everyone else saw anyway. Carl looked out and saw represented there all the people he had known, all the people who mattered in his life. He was doing this for them and for his crew, now long gone except himself and Jack Jilllson. He also saw those he now considered his family; his fellow volunteers from the local Combat Air Museum, his friend the chaplain from the Ex-POW Chapter, his neighbor who had been so faithful in helping him do things around the house in his declining years, his trusted financial advisor, and his pastor. Kirby could not be there that day, but he and Heidi had called to wish him luck. Carl had told his nephews this entire story, over the years, in letter after letter to them. He wanted them to know. He wanted them to remember. His nephews understood how important this day was for him. The staff had helped Marguerite dress for the occasion, and had done her hair and painted her fingernails. She was in her wheelchair at his side, and she still looked beautiful. He was proud to have her at his side, where she belonged. For her part, she was beaming, looking at him with love and with pride. Yes, it was going to be a good day. He drew a deep breath, and began to speak. It was a shining moment.

The Commander from the VFW came in to meet him after the speech. Carl was exhausted, but he wasn't about to let anyone know. He sat up in bed, showing no sign of what that exertion cost him. He shook hands with the man and they exchanged pleasantries. Then Carl proceeded to tell the man about Joseph Sawicki. It was his last shot, he knew, his last effort on Sawicki's behalf. He made the man promise to look into it, which the man solemnly agreed to do. The man left proudly carrying an autographed copy of Carl's book in his hand. It was the last book Carl would ever sign. Carl had also made Kirby and his pastor, along with many others, promise to him that they would continue to seek the Medal of Honor for Sawicki. He was not going to leave this world without making sure the fight for Sawicki's honor would continue. He lay back, spent, sure that he now had done everything he could do for Joseph. It was too late for him to do more.

****

Carl was dreaming. It was World War II again; only this time the Dark Horse was headed for sure death in the icy waters of the English Channel. He was fighting the plane with all his might, trying to bring the nose up out of the death dive. For some reason, Marguerite's voice was coming over the radio, "Don't leave me Carl, you must fight, you can't leave me!" He renewed his efforts to reverse the dive, pulling back on the stick with everything he had. "Addison, Molnar, where are you damn it, help me with this." The curse words streamed from his mouth. He was losing the battle, he was going to go down into that water and drown …. He must fight it; he must not go into that dark water … where was everybody?

****

He stirred and looked around. Marguerite was sleeping in her bed on his left, one of the ladies from church was sitting next to him on his right, waiting. He knew they would not leave his side now until the end came. The pastor, who had been there most of the day, was gone now, but he knew she would be back sooner or later. They should probably call Kirby and Heidi; they would have a lot of work to do soon. He left them in charge of his affairs, knowing they would do everything in their power to act according to his wishe. It was so hard to breathe, there was so much weight on his chest. He reached for Marguerite's hand, found it, held her delicate fingers close between his long frail ones. The love of his life. How had he ever been so lucky as to find her? He was tired, so tired. Then mercifully sleep overcame him. The world went dark …

****

Suddenly he was standing next to his bed, and to his astonishment he realized that he was watching the nurses do CPR on his body, as Marguerite cried next to him. It was as if he were watching a movie. It was hard to see Marguerite so distraught. Then the nurse was on the phone to his nephew, the one who was like his own son, even though he had never had one. It did Carl's heart good to have someone he could leave his medals to, and he had left explicit instructions to that effect, so there would be no doubt as to where he wanted them to go. It was odd; Carl could hear Kirby's voice as if he were in the room with him. He sounded like he was choking too. Carl knew the boy was faced with making a difficult decision in a grave situation.

"How bad is it?" Kirby asked.

"It's bad," the nurse replied.

"Stop."

Yes, boy, stop, it is time," Carl thought "You've done well and I am proud of you. Let it go. It is time for me to go."

Carl turned away from the scene before him suddenly aware that it was not a place he belonged anymore. As he turned he felt his leg turn with him, something it hadn't done since he had been hit by a jeep in 1943 ... then he looked down and realized with a start he was in his Air Force uniform again. In a daze, he held his hands out in front of him and saw the hands of a young man, one who was vital and could handle any airplane they wanted to send his way. He laughed in surprise. He turned back one last time and saw Marguerite again, only this time he saw her through the eyes of a young man looking at a beautiful young woman. "Goodbye love, I will see you soon." He bent over and gave her a gentle kiss on her tear stained cheek, one she felt as a breath of wind on her skin. Then, he turned to leave for good. He headed out into what he thought was a deserted hallway, but as he headed for the door, he became aware of a man stepping out of the shadows, dressed in the flight suit of a B-17 tail gunner. To Carl it seemed the air around the man's body shimmered in the dim lighting of the hallway.

"Major Fyler," the man said, "It's me. I am here for you."

Carl's memory reeled. "I should know that voice," he thought. Then, as if Carl had spoken out loud the man said "Its me. It's Joseph."

Sawicki? Joseph Sawicki? Handsome and whole? How could that be? But of course Carl knew. He knew he had passed into the next world, and now he understood. Sawicki had come to escort him home.

"My God Sawicki, it's so good to see you again."

"Yes Sir. You too. We have much to talk about, but later. Now we must go. The rest of the men are waiting for you."

"Of course. Let's go."

Joseph R. Sawicki smiled, pulled himself to attention, and saluted. Carl returned the salute, and then the two men went through the door of the nursing home out into the brilliant light of the courtyard.

As the door shut behind them, the grandfather clock in the lobby of the nursing home began to chime. As the light from outside receded, the old clock chimed 11 times.

It was on the 11th day of the 11th month at the 11th hour that Carl John Fyler walked into the great beyond.

From The Authors:

Carl pressed on with his quest for many years on behalf of all veterans living and deceased. He assisted many heart broken widows who came to him when the system failed them. Carl's frustration with the very people assigned by the federal government to see that these American veterans and patriots were taken care of properly under the law was endless and overwhelming. Carl put country first while some appeared to be putting it last. For reasons unknown to this day many within the United States government displayed a lack of respect and dignity toward these veterans and Carl himself. This is well documented in the archive of hundreds of letters Carl wrote to his three nephews over many years. They understood his efforts. He was very proud to let them know when he was successful and many times showed his frustration and pain when he was unsuccessful. The crucial 64 year battle on behalf of 20-year-old Polish-American tail gunner Joseph R. Sawicki is just one example of Carl's dedication to the cause. He preserved the Sawicki Story and has since passed the fiery torch to family and friends to continue the fight to Washington D.C. to assure Joseph R. Sawicki is properly honored and respected not only in the United States but around the world. God willing this mission shall be completed.

A special thanks goes out to the men and women who gave of their time and did put forth the effort to assist Carl and the many American veterans. You know who you are and so do we.

Major Carl J. Fyler along with all the American military veterans current and past have placed their country first and made the ultimate sacrifice, many with their lives.

Please show them your appreciation at all times and provide them with the dignity and understanding they deserve.

11-11: The Carl Fyler Story was written for the sole purpose to give the reader an up close personal look at just one veteran who loved his country and what it stands for.

Thank you,
Karl Webb and Ann Norlin
August, 2011

Resources

Primary Resources
Diaries, writings, and letters of Maj. Carl J. Fyler
Recorded interviews with Carl J. Fyler
Recorded interview with Jack Jillson, last living member of the Fyler Crew.
Interview with Rex Gary
300 Polish Squadron RAF Archives
Fyler Family Association

Books
1. Donald L. Miller, *"Masters of the Air,"* (New York, Simon and Schuster, 2006)
2. Brian D. O'Neil, *"Half a Wing, Three Engines and a Prayer,"* (New York, McGraw Hill, 1999)
3. Carl J. Fyler, *"Staying Alive,"* (Leavenworth KS, J. H. Johnston III, 1995)
4. Carruth, Gorton. *"The Encyclopedia of American Facts and Dates"*. 10th Ed. New York: Harper Collins Publishers.

Internet
1. 303rd Heavy Bomb Group - www.303rdbg.com
2. 8th Air Force Historical Society - www.8thafhs.org
3. Stalag Luft 1 - www.merkki.com
4. American Battlefield Preservation - www.nps.gov/history/hps/abpp
5. Union Regimental Index - www.civilwararchive.com/regim.htm
6. World War II History - www.worldwariihistory.info
7. Wikipedia - www.wikipedia.org
8. Historynet - www.historynet.com
9. American Ex-POWs - www.axpow.org
10. Combat Air Museum - www.combatairmuseum.org

www.ingramcontent.com/pod-product-compliance
Lightning Source LLC
Chambersburg PA
CBHW071725090426
42738CB00009B/1886